BONES OF FAERIE

Janni Lee Simner

Cholla Bear Press

Tucson, Arizona

For Larry: 3333, 4556, 5645.
But you knew that, right?

Also by Janni Lee Simner

The Bones of Faerie trilogy
  Bones of Faerie
  Faerie Winter
  Faerie After

Thief Eyes

Tiernay West, Professional Adventurer

*Doing What You Love: Practical Strategies
for Living a Creative Life*

✑ Chapter 1 ✑

I had a sister once. She was a beautiful baby, eyes silver as moonlight off the river at night. From the hour of her birth she was long-limbed and graceful, faerie-pale hair clear as glass from Before, so pale you could almost see through to the soft skin beneath.

My father was a sensible man. He set her out on the hillside that very night, though my mother wept and even old Jayce argued against it. "If the faerie folk want her, let them take her," Father said. "If not, the fault's theirs for not claiming one of their own." He left my sister, and he never looked back.

I did. I crept out before dawn to see whether the faeries had really come. They hadn't, but some wild creature had.

One glance was all I could take. I turned and

ran for home, telling no one where I'd been.

We were lucky that time, I knew. I'd heard tales of a woman who bore a child with a voice high and sweet as a bird's song—and with the sharp claws to match. No one questioned that baby's father when he set the child out to die, far from our town, far from where his wife lay dying, her insides torn and bleeding.

Magic was never meant for our world, Father said, and of course I'd agreed, though the War had ended and the faerie folk returned to their own places before I was born. If only they'd never stirred from those places—but it was no use thinking that way.

Besides, I'd heard often enough that our town did better than most. We knew the rules. Don't touch any stone that glows with faerie light, or that light will burn you fiercer than any fire. Don't venture out alone into the dark, or the darkness will swallow you whole. And cast out the magic born among you, before it can turn on its parents.

Towns had died for not understanding that much. My father was a sensible man.

But the memory of my sister's bones, cracked and bloody in the moonlight, haunts me still.

❧ Chapter 2 ❧

Three weeks after my sister's birth I hurried through town, my breath puffing into the chilly air and an empty bucket banging against my hip. The sun was just above the horizon, turning layers of pink cloud to gold. Most of the other townsfolk were already in the fields, their morning chores done.

I walked quickly past the row of white-washed houses I'd known all my life. Their windows were firmly shuttered or else tacked with old nylon against the cold. My gaze lingered a moment on the gap among those houses, but then I rushed on, thinking about how I'd overslept again that morning, not waking until Father had slammed the door as he left the house—deliberately loud, a warning to me. I'd already been sleeping badly since Father had cast my sister out, my dreams filled with restless shadows and a baby's cries. Then a week ago Mom left us. Since then I'd hardly slept at all, save in the early hours for just long enough to make it hard to wake again.

I passed the last of our town's tended houses; passed, too, the houses we didn't tend, which were little more than tangles of ragweed with splintered wood poking through. At the fork in the path I caught a whiff of metallic steam from Jayce's forge. I headed left. The path skirted the edge of the cornfields, then narrowed. Maples and sycamores grew along its edges, draped with wild grape. Green tendrils snaked out from the grapevines as I passed. I knew those vines sought skin to root in, so I kept to the path's center, where they couldn't reach. Plants used to be bound firmly to the places where they grew, but that was before the faerie folk came to our world.

No one knew why they came. No one even knew what they looked like. The War happened too fast, and the televisions people once had for speaking to one another all died the first day. Some said the faerie folk looked like trees, with

5

gnarled arms and peeling brown skin. Others said they were dark winged shadows, with only their clear hair and silver eyes visible as they attacked us. Hair like that remained a sure sign a child was tainted with magic.

But whatever the faerie folk looked like, everyone agreed they were monsters. Because once they were here they turned their magic against us, ordering the trees to seek human flesh and the stones to burn with deadly light. Even after the War ended and the faerie folk left this world, the magic they'd set loose lingered, killing still.

The path ended at the river, though another path, narrower still, continued both ways along its near bank. I clambered down a short rocky slope and dipped my bucket into the water. Our well had silted up again, so the river was the only place to draw water for cooking and chores.

When the bucket was full I drew it out again, set it down, and cupped my hands for a drink. As I did a wind picked up, and I shivered. Mom would be cold, out alone on a morning like this. I knew better than to hope she yet lived, but still I whispered as I dipped my hands into the bucket, "Where are you? Where?"

Light flashed. A sickly sweet scent like tree sap filled the air. I jerked my hands back, but I couldn't turn away.

The water in the bucket glowed like steel in the sun, holding my gaze. The wind died around me. From somewhere very far away, Mom called my name.

I grabbed a stone and threw it into the bucket. There was a sound like shattering ice, and then the water within was merely water, clouded by ripples and mud from the rock, nothing more.

My mother was gone. Why couldn't I accept that? I must have imagined her voice, just as I'd imagined the way the water had seemed to glow.

Yet I'd seen light like that once before.

The night my sister was born—the night I'd fled from the hillside, where I never should have been—I'd seen flashes at the edges of my sight, like lightning, though the night was clear. I'd ignored them and kept running, calling the name my mother had chosen but only once been able to use. "Rebecca! *Rebecca!*" My throat and chest had tightened, but I couldn't seem to stop.

The night Mom left there'd been lightning, too, more ordinary flickers from an autumn storm. That light had illuminated her tear-streaked face as she slipped quietly into my room. I reached for her, but she drew away, clutching the necklace she always wore — a metal disk on a chain, laced with narrow veins. I drifted back to sleep, thinking I'd only dreamed it, but when I woke in the morning, Mom was gone.

"She knew the rules," Father had said when she failed to return by nightfall. I searched his face for some hint of the grief he must have felt and saw a tightness around his jaw and eyes, nothing more. He knew as well as I how unlikely Mom was to have survived a night alone in the dark, yet he didn't cry. He said there was no sense wasting tears on things you couldn't change.

I did my own crying alone in the dark, where no one could see. Why would Mom leave without telling where she'd gone? I would have gone with her. I'm good with a knife and a bow. I'd have kept watch for her or done whatever else she needed.

I gripped the bucket's handle with both hands and climbed back up the slope. As I reached the top I saw Matthew emerging from the path between river and town. His fair hair was pulled back in a ragged ponytail, but as usual it had escaped and fallen loose around his ears. He smiled when he saw me — an easy, comfortable smile — but I looked away. I didn't find being around Matthew comfortable at all.

"Hey, Liza. Your dad's looking for you." Matthew rubbed at the jagged white scar around his left wrist, and his smile faltered a little. "Wondering why you're not to work yet."

I glanced at the sky. The sun shone like tarnished silver through layers of gray. When had it risen so high? Sweat trickled down my neck and made my sweater itch against my clammy skin. How long had I stared into the water? Had magic held me transfixed while time flowed on all around me?

No. I was tired, that was all. I'd lost track of

the time.

"Need any help?" Matthew asked.

"I'm fine." I walked past him, back toward the town. I'd pay for being so late, but that was none of Matthew's concern. He came up beside me anyway, matching my pace with his own loping gait. He shoved his hands into the pockets of his deerskin jacket and said, "Your dad's in one of his moods."

Of course he was. I kept walking. The sun grew brighter, turning the maple and sycamore leaves deep green. Mom said before the War, leaves had changed color in autumn, first blazing fiery shades of yellow and red, then falling softly to earth, leaving behind bare branches that shivered beneath winter snows. It would take a fire now to make any tree release its grip so easily.

Matthew lifted his head and sniffed the air. The scent of leaf mold was heavy around us. "I can go with you," he offered. "Maybe if I'm with you, Ian won't ..." Matthew let the words trail off.

"You can go *away*." Water sloshed over the edges of the bucket. Bad enough Father would likely lash me for being late. I didn't need for

Matthew to follow and see. He stayed with me, though, right up until we reached the edge of the fields. There, he hesitated and glanced at me. I scowled. Matthew shrugged uneasily and turned away, heading off along a side path between fields of corn. The stalks' long leaves rustled as he went by. In the distance, corn ears moaned as townsfolk pulled them free. The corn had grown well this year, and the squash and beans, too. They'd all fought our harvesting, and we had the bruises to show for it, but come winter we would eat well.

I continued back into town. This time when I reached the gap among the houses, I couldn't help it. I stopped, thinking of how Matthew smiled as if no magic had ever touched his life. I knew better. We all did.

Matthew's little brother, Cam, had called blackberry brambles into their house nearly two years ago now, though we didn't know he'd called them at first. We just knew we woke to the sound of Cam's parents screaming.

All the townsfolk came running, and by the lanterns we brought with us we saw Cam's house swarming with thorny blackberry stems.

11

Wood walls creaked and snapped as the screams fell to silence, yet even as the house collapsed we heard Cam laughing. We couldn't get him or his parents out. We could only burn the house down to keep the blackberry bushes from attacking the houses around it as well.

Everyone thought Matthew had died with his family, until a few hours later when he appeared at the edge of town. His clothes were gone, his skin was crossed with ragged scrapes, and his wrist still bled where the thorny stems had grabbed him. At first he was too dazed to speak. Later he told us what had happened, though he kept insisting Cam hadn't done it on purpose. His brother was just a little kid, Matthew said, throwing a little-kid tantrum. Cam didn't know a blackberry plant had taken root beneath his porch. No one knew, for all that we checked for new growth as often as we could. Yet the plant had heard Cam's cries. It had broken through the porch and headed straight for him. Father said Matthew was a coward for running away instead of going for help. He said even a few extra minutes might have saved Cam and his family. I didn't know what to think, just as I didn't know quite what to say to Matthew after that. Mostly I didn't say anything at all. After two years, it had become a habit.

Later Brianna the midwife admitted she'd seen a few clear strands in Cam's hair earlier that year, meaning it'd likely been Cam's magic that had called the plant, and not simple bad luck that it had come. Until then we'd thought magic showed up either at birth or not at all, but now we were more careful. Cam and Matthew's grandmother Kate gathered the town's children together regularly to check our hair for magic, just as she checked for lice and fleas. As far as Kate could tell, though, Cam had been the only one.

I turned away from the empty space where Matthew's family had died and hurried on to my own house. As I started up the creaking steps, I saw a yellow dandelion growing beside them. I set my bucket down and tugged at the green stem. A thorn sliced my palm. I brought it to my mouth, cursing the spiteful plant, then took the knife from my belt and cut the dandelion free with a single stroke. "I'll be back for your roots," I promised as I hefted the bucket again and stepped inside.

A streak of amber fur leaped across the living room. I dropped the bucket as Tallow, my old yellow barn cat, landed in my arms. In spite of myself I smiled and scratched her behind the ears.

"Where were you?" I whispered. Tallow had lived in our town since I was small. When she was a kitten she'd sneak beneath the covers with me at night, until Father found out. "She's no use as a mouser if she spends her days lazing on feather mattresses," he'd said. Tallow kept sneaking in despite my best efforts, though. Until last night, when she'd gone missing and I went out calling for her, afraid she'd left this world at last. I called until my throat grew itchy and tight, but Tallow didn't come. Yet now she purred as if she'd never been gone. I held her close a moment, then gently carried her outside and set her down on the stairs. Tallow looked up at me, green eyes large, as if hurt that I'd even consider setting her out. "You have to earn your keep," I told her. "Just like the rest of us."

Tallow yawned, telling me what she thought of that notion, and curled up on the top step to sleep.

I went back inside and carried the water past our couch — its cushions torn and patched and torn again — past a fireplace filled with cold ash, and into the kitchen. Plastic bins of corn and dried meat lined the kitchen walls. Their labels were faded beyond reading, but like old nylon, old plastic endured. It was one of the things that had best survived the War. I set the bucket down beside the sink.

Light flashed off the sink's metal surface, even though the kitchen windows were shuttered. The light turned bright and clear, reflecting back my own face. Ice-pale hair tumbled over my shoulders, flowing like water into my outstretched hands —

"No!" I wrenched my gaze away and tore at my hair. The strands that came free were as black as they'd ever been, dark as rich soil, dark as a moonless night. Yet there was a hint of something paler at their roots. I sank to my knees and pressed my face to the cool, crumbling kitchen tiles. Had some of Rebecca's magic lingered on the hillside? Had that magic found me, even as I ran? Was I the one faerie-cursed now?

My hands shook. Whether I spoke of this or not, sooner or later someone would find out and destroy me and the magic both. Or worse, I would destroy them, just as Matthew's little brother had done. Magic always did harm sooner or later. I drew a shuddering breath and stumbled to my feet.

When I turned, Father stood in the doorway, watching me.

❧ Chapter 3 ❧

Words froze in my throat as I stared at my father. Had he seen the light in the sink, the paleness in my hair? *Cast out the magic born among you.* Yet I was no babe to set out in the night. Father had told me often enough how he'd have dealt with Cam had the boy lived: "With a single stroke across the throat, swift and deep." Father killed deer that way after the hunt, his knife cutting so fast there was never any pain.

"You're late, Liza." Father stared at me through hard gray eyes.

I let out a breath. I'd forgotten he might have ordinary reasons for anger, too.

"Why are you late?" His voice was a growl at the back of his throat. He crossed the room with a few quick strides. I wished I were like

Tallow, who could disappear when she didn't wish to be found. "Where were you?" Father demanded.

"Ou-out," I stammered. "Getting water ..." My words trailed to silence. We both knew getting water ought not to have taken so long.

"There's work to be done." Father's eyes flashed like iron in Jayce's forge, but his voice remained low. "People who don't work don't eat."

"I know. I'm sorry. I—"

He slapped me so hard and fast, tears came to my eyes. I blinked them back even as he grabbed my arm. "People who don't work starve. Don't you understand that?"

I said nothing. I feared any wrong word might betray the magic that had delayed me.

"Five lashes, girl."

I knew better than to run. Running would only make him angrier. Instead I turned my back, lifted my sweater, and bowed my head against the pain I knew would come. Silently Father drew his belt. The first blow hit—I fought not to cry out. The second broke skin and sent stabs of pain down my back. I bit my lip and tasted blood.

With each lash Father spoke quiet angry words about faerie fire and human death, about people starving and ungrateful children who didn't understand. My back throbbed. Three, I counted. Four. With the fifth lash a sob burst from my lips.

"Weak," Father said as he tied his belt back in place. "You'd have died during the War, Liza. Remember that."

I nodded, not trusting myself to speak.

"Now pull yourself together and join me in the fields. No more delays."

I listened as his deliberate steps crossed the house and the outside door shut firmly behind him. I let my knees give way and sank, trembling, to the floor, sweater falling back into place. More sobs came, along with a throbbing pain that grew with every breath. If Mom were here I might have run to her so that she could hold me and whisper some of the pain away. Mom didn't think me weak or slow. She didn't think that at fifteen I was too old to beg for comfort like a child.

How could she have left me without a word?

I staggered to my feet and headed back outside. I'd barely made it down the stairs when the pain slid up a notch and I fell to my knees again. I reached around and touched my back. My hand came away sticky with blood. It was worse than usual. I tried to pull the wool away to feel the skin beneath, but wool and blood and skin stuck together. Redness shimmered before my eyes.

I felt something like old sandpaper against my cheek. Tallow licked my face. Her rough tongue hurt. I pushed her away. She mewed in protest.

I couldn't work like this. Father didn't believe in numbing pain — he kept none of Jayce's whiskey on hand. I forced myself to my feet and stumbled down the path toward Kate's door, Tallow at my heels. Matthew's grand-mother didn't have whiskey, either, but she did have a cupboard full of teas and herbs. She'd have something for the pain. And she'd be home: her knees had grown too weak for her to help with the harvest.

I hesitated, then knocked and nudged the door open just as Kate called at me to enter. She sat on a stool in front of her loom, her hands in her lap as she stared at a half-finished bolt of reddish-brown cloth. Her long gray hair was twisted into a tidy bun. Across the room, a low fire burned in her fireplace.

"Hello, Liza." She turned, smiling, to face me, but her smile tightened into a hard line as she looked me over. "What did he do this time?"

"It's nothing." Even shaking my head hurt. Bad enough I'd angered Father; I shouldn't have come here and let Kate see. I never let anyone see, for all that Kate always seemed to know anyway. "I just wanted to borrow some tea." My voice came out hoarser than I'd expected.

Kate stood, wincing at the weight on her knees. A wave of dizziness made me stagger. Kate laid her hand on my arm, leading me toward the couch. I sighed and sat down. Kate gently pulled the sweater away from my skin and over my head. She drew a sharp breath, ordered me to lie on my stomach, and examined my back with gentle, probing fingers, pausing each time I flinched. I tried to sit up, but she laid a firm hand on my shoulder. She disappeared into the kitchen, returning a few moments later with a teakettle in one hand and a basket full of clay bottles and coarse bandages in the other. She placed the kettle on the fire, then knelt by my side and soaked a bandage with liquid. If her knees ached now, she gave no sign, saying only, "This might sting a little, but we have to clean you up before infection sets in."

The liquid didn't sting—it burned. I tried not to cry out, but again couldn't help myself. Unlike Father, Kate said nothing, just ran her fingers through my hair, a little like Mom had done when I was small.

After the burning liquid came a thicker salve. Numbing coolness dulled the pain. Kate wrapped bandages over the salve. She warned me to keep the skin covered, then helped me sit up and offered me a clean sweater. I pulled it on as the kettle began to boil. Kate poured me some tea. I sipped the bitter liquid as she looked me over, her mouth still set in that tight line. "Better?"

I nodded. "Thank you. I can work now." Even my voice seemed steadier. I tried to stand, but again Kate stopped me.

An unreadable expression crossed the old woman's face. "Wait here," she said abruptly, and disappeared down the hall. I heard the stairs creak as she climbed. She mostly slept downstairs and let Matthew, who lived with her now, do the climbing.

I finished the tea and stood, with less pain this time. I walked slowly around the room, looking at Kate's colorful wall hangings and at a bookcase filled with yellowed volumes. As I stepped past her loom something bright glinted beside it. One of the hangings had fallen askew. I drew it back and saw a rectangle of glass, taller than I was, set in a frame decorated with gold flowers. No, not glass—a mirror. I'd never seen a mirror intact before. They'd all been broken during the War; no one ever said why. I'd hardly seen glass at all, save for shards clinging to empty window frames and a few old drinking glasses. The mirror cast back an impossible, perfect reflection, clear as if I'd stepped outside of myself. The girl who stared back at me seemed a stranger: dark hair falling around her shoulders, dark eyes large in her sun-browned face, leather pants grown short about her ankles. I turned away, embarrassed by my own shy gaze. Yet after only a moment I glanced back, wanting to check what I'd seen, to remember who I was.

As I looked, the image in the mirror wavered and flowed away in rivulets of light. In the brightness left behind, I saw —

Myself, not in Kate's home but by the river that morning, my hand poised above a bucket filled with light —

My mother, hair tied back from her weary face, slipping out into the night —

A pale-haired young man, clearly touched by magic, walking through a sun-drenched forest. He showed no fear as a hawk flew through the leaves and landed on his outstretched wrist —

My sister, breathing her first cries while the midwife shook her head —

A girl walking through the night, her hair trailing in the wind. A girl who, for just a moment, turned, revealing a face like mine, only her hair was streaked pale as glass —

I tore my gaze from the mirror and threw my hands up to my face. Faerie magic. Cursed magic.

Magic showing me the past, showing me things I'd never seen. My hands shook as I pressed them against my eyes. There was no denying now that magic had taken root somewhere inside me, perhaps on the night I'd gone out after Rebecca, perhaps weeks, months, or years before.

I heard footsteps behind me and turned to see Kate clutching a small jar in one hand. "Liza." Her soft voice reminded me of the touch of her fingers through my hair.

Had she seen my pale roots? Had she seen the visions in the mirror? I didn't know. But I did know that Cam's magic had destroyed Kate's family. Would my magic kill, too?

No, not if I could help it. No one would die from my magic but me. I turned from Kate's pitying gaze and ran. "Wait!" Kate stumbled after me, but she was too slow. I fled from my town and the fields I'd known all my life. I fled into the woods and didn't look back.

✌ Chapter 4 ✆

When Father taught me to hunt he said, "Never show fear. Animals and plants can sense fear in your every move. They can smell fear with your every breath."

I'd asked him whether that was because of the War, but he'd only laughed softly. "No, Liza. That much has always been true. Difference now is that hunter and hunted look much the same. You can never be sure which is which, not until the hunt is through." Plants hadn't been among the hunters Before, but Father didn't need to say that.

I didn't feel like much of a hunter: not when I reached the river and followed it at a run, not hours later when Kate's salve had worn off and my throbbing back forced me to a walk, not now as the sun dipped below the horizon. Tallow trotted along beside me, unafraid. She'd followed as I fled, and though I'd tried to send her home, in truth I was glad of her company. The cat had ridden on my shoulders much of the day, until they'd grown too sore. I'd taught her to ride there years ago, when she was a kitten.

I kept to the center of the path, barely out of reach of the ragweed along its edges, but it wasn't the ragweed that worried me most. Father had taught me well—I knew I was being followed. My pursuer had been with me the past mile, maybe longer. Ferns and brambles rustled as they shied away from distant footfalls. Ash and redbud and oak whispered softly as those footfalls passed by. And I felt something watching me from within the deepening shadows, felt it with a certainty that made cold sweat trickle down my neck.

Don't venture out alone into the dark, or the darkness will swallow you whole. Even when the sun shone, a tree could take a grown man down if it had taste enough for blood. When the sun set, shadows gathered around the trees and around the other plants, too, not always, but often enough. Not just the ordinary shadows that gather everywhere as the sun gets low — these were darker, with a slow thickness like tree sap, and they didn't go away once the sun set. Even in the dark, shadow vines crept along the ground and shadow branches slashed at the air. Those tree shadows cut deeper than ordinary branches and brambles. Jayce still walked with a limp because a pokeweed shadow had cut him to the bone when he stayed out too late on a hunt.

Yet I thought what hunted me now was human. Someone from my town, sent to find me. I thought — but couldn't be sure. I shivered in the fading light. If plants and animals could smell fear, mine left them an easy trail. A few wild grape-vines crept tentatively toward the path. If I called them the way Cam had called, would they sense my magic and come to me? I walked faster, beyond their reach.

Something moved among the trees, closer than before. Tallow's ears perked forward. The some-thing rustled through the brush, veering toward the river. Toward me. Its steps were faster, more sure than they'd been before.

I ran once more. The rustling thing ran, too,

matching my pace. The path between forest and river narrowed. If only I could leap above water and wood into the evening sky, the way the airplanes did Before — but I could merely run harder as the water grew near.

Mom sang stories from Before sometimes, faerie songs from a time when only a very few people knew the faerie folk were real. In some of those songs running water stopped magic, just as cold iron did. Iron hadn't helped the airplanes — magic brought them down long ago. But water was different. If the water flowed swiftly enough, neither plants nor magic could get a hold in its depths. I turned and ran off the trail, through a small hickory grove, and down the rocky bank into the river. I gasped as icy water washed over my boots and soaked through my wool socks, but kept moving into deeper water. Mud sucked at my feet and I stumbled, struggling to right myself against the current.

Even as I did, the water around me went abruptly still. That water had risen nearly to my waist. It soaked through my clothes and chilled my skin. I stumbled again and stared. The air had gone very quiet. Near the far shore the river flowed on, but around me nothing moved. Even my pursuer was silent. Tallow stared at me from the near bank, silent as well.

A flash of light drew my gaze downward. The water around me began to shine like a giant mirror. I fled that magic the only way I could, by shutting my eyes and diving beneath the surface. Perhaps if I didn't look, the magic would pass me by and seek someone else to root in instead.

Or I could stay beneath the surface. I could let myself drown and hope the magic died with me — but even as I thought that, I burst into the air, coughing and gasping for breath. My boots were heavy with water, and my wet clothes clung to my cold skin. The river around me had stopped glowing. I swam for shore and as I did the current started up again, pulling at my clothes and dragging me down. I swam harder, then stood and staggered on. Another few steps and I would be on land.

A rock slipped beneath me and I fell into a hole of deeper water. I reached out blindly even as my head went under. My arms and legs ached with weariness. I really was about to drown, whether I wanted to or not.

Someone grasped my wrists, hard.

That firm grip was enough for me to find solid footing and break through the surface once more. I clambered, splashing onto the bank, gulping air. Behind me the river murmured quietly, just a river, nothing more.

"Liza."

I looked up. "Matthew." His hair was coming loose, and a dead maple leaf had gotten caught in it.

"You nearly drowned." His voice shook. Sweat trickled down his face in spite of the chilly air. "Are you all right?"

Kate must have sent him after me. She ought to have known better than to send anyone. I stood, shivering. Tallow had moved out of range of my splashing. She licked the mud from her fur.

Twilight cast shadows on Matthew's pale face. He ran his hand over his hair, found the leaf, and drew it free. "I brought you food," he said as he threw the leaf into the water. "Dry clothes. Flint and steel for a fire."

"No." My teeth chattered. My feet were ice, my fingertips tingling. "You need — to go. To get — away — from me."

"Liza." Matthew's voice was low but firm, a little like his grandmother's. "I'm going to gather wood for a fire. You'll feel better once you're warm. Okay?"

Nothing could make this okay, but Matthew reached into the backpack beside him, pulled out a blanket, and draped it over my shoulders. Next he drew out a clay jug filled with oil and used a spark from his flint to light the wick within. I drew closer to that small circle of light.

Matthew took out a torch next, lit it from the lamp, and slung a nylon bag for gathering wood over his shoulder. He left me the lamp and retreated into the forest, his torch flickering among the trees. The night shifted from gray to black, and the moon rose as he searched the ground for dead wood.

Didn't he know better than to gather firewood alone at night? Didn't he know better than to risk his life for a magic-cursed girl?

But maybe Kate hadn't told him about my

magic. I'd have to tell him as soon as he returned. Matthew didn't deserve to suffer from whatever harm my magic might bring.

*   *   *

Matthew gripped the branch he used to stir the fire. By the orange firelight, I could see his fear, the fear Father taught me always to hide. It showed in the hunch of his shoulders and the way the branch trembled in his hand. Between us embers cracked and popped, the green at the heart of even fallen wood slow to burn. Tallow was curled beside the fire, asleep. At the edges of the path, branches bent away from the flames, fearing their heat. I scanned the dark leaves for tree shadows but saw none.

Something howled in the night. The cat opened her eyes and raised one ear. Wild dogs, I thought. Trees and their shadows weren't the only danger here.

Matthew lifted a metal mug from the fire, holding it carefully by the leather-wrapped handle. "Here. You need to get something warm into you."

Wearing dry clothes, wrapped in Matthew's

blanket, I'd finally stopped shivering. Steam rose from the mug, the scent of mint and lemon balm mixing with that of smoke and wet wool. Some night creature screamed and fell silent in a flurry of leaves. The wild dogs howled again, a little closer. Matthew set the mug down at my feet and poked the fire with his branch. Sparks leaped into the air, turned to ash, and softly fell. Matthew looked at me as if unsure whether to speak.

I looked away. "You need to go," I said.

Matthew laughed uneasily. "And venture out alone into the dark? What would your father say?" I think he meant it as a joke, but I saw nothing funny about it. A moth flew toward the fire and through the flames. It flew out again with the veins in its gray wings glowing orange. Moths were drawn to light and always took some away with them when they found it.

I stood and pulled the blanket around me like a cloak, ignoring the pain that stiffened my back. "Cast out the magic born among you," I said slowly, "before it can turn on its parents."

Matthew took a small metal pot from his

pack and silently filled it with water from a plastic bottle. Tallow stretched and sniffed the air. Matthew lifted his head, as if whatever Tallow smelled, he smelled, too.

"You know what happened to my sister." The wind picked up with a mournful sound like a baby's cry.

Matthew's frightened look hardened into something else. His eyes narrowed as he set the pot on the fire. "What your father did. He had no right." Matthew's voice was low and fierce. His lips drew back from his teeth.

"He had every right. And now it's happening to me."

"I know." Matthew took cornmeal from a leather pouch and added it to the pot. He lifted his head, and his gray eyes seemed to reflect distant light—not firelight, more like the moon rising through the trees.

I looked away from him, down to the bubbling pot. Light reflected off its metal surface, and as I watched, the metal grew bright—just like the water and the mirror behind Kate's loom. I tried to turn away, but my gaze was held fast, and in the brightness I saw —

A pale young man walking through a forest, not alone this time but with a dark-haired young woman — my age — smiling by his side. Sun turned the leaves green-gold and made the air around them shimmer —

A land of steel and glass, of towers and sharp angles. A sky the color of dried blood. Shadows reaching like grasping branches for the towers. The towers shuddered and crumbled to dust, while beyond them a broad river flowed swiftly on, its waters muddy and deep —

Mom gazing at me through water, through a curving wall of silver light. Mom whispering, "Lizzy, my baby, my girl. Stay hidden, Liza; stay safe — "

I stared at her sad eyes, reached for her hand —

— and screamed as hot metal burned me. Matthew yanked my arm from the heated pot, even as I fought to reach for that heat — for my mother — once more.

"Mom!" I cried, but he didn't let go. Blisters rose on my fingers. I felt pain, but it seemed a distant thing, less real than the images I'd seen.

Matthew held me until I stopped struggling and sank wearily beside the fire. He pressed a cool cloth against my burned fingers. The metal pot reflected orange firelight, nothing more. Mom was gone.

Cornmeal boiled over into the fire, but Matthew didn't move to pull the pot away. Tallow butted my knee with her head, and I absently shoved her back. "What did you see?" Matthew asked.

I didn't want to put the images into words. That would make them more real — or less. I said nothing.

Matthew shook his head, dismissing my silence. "Gram thought you saw something in her mirror, even though she couldn't see it for herself. I couldn't see anything, either, but only someone in the grip of magic would reach toward a fire as if she didn't know it was there."

"How would you know?" My blisters throbbed. My back still ached. How badly would I have been burned if Matthew hadn't pulled me away?

In the woods the howling grew louder. Matthew hesitated, then said, "You're not the only person I've known with magic."

"Yes, but all the others are *dead*." The words came out before I could stop them. My sister. His brother. An unnamed baby with a bird's sharp claws. Other babies, born to other women, one every few years since the War.

Matthew's gaze was sharp, nothing like the smiling boy I knew back home. "When Cam died I swore he'd be the last. I swore no one else would die for magic if I could help it."

"Well, you failed, then, didn't you?" My voice came out harsher than I'd expected. *Father had no choice*, I thought. *He was protecting us all.* I turned away from Matthew.

Even as I did, something brown and furred leaped out of the night, knocking me to the ground. I fumbled for my knife and slashed upward, ignoring pain as blisters burst. Teeth snapped, ripping wool and leather. Howls and yips rang all around. My knife struck deep, and blood splattered my face. I struggled for breath as I pulled the knife away, looking up into the bloodshot yellow eyes of a wild dog. Claws slashed at my cheek. I rolled away, back throbbing, arms protecting my neck, bracing for the bite of teeth against skin.

Instead the creature whined, deep in its throat. Abruptly it turned and ran, tail between its legs. Other dogs ran after it, a whole pack. What could scare a pack of wild dogs?

I heard panting behind me and felt hot breath on my arms. Clutching my knife, I stood and turned.

I saw — not a dog, not quite. Its eyes were too bright, its teeth too sharp, its fur as much silver as gray. The creature snarled as it watched the pack retreat. Its lips were drawn back, its ears and tail erect. Blood dripped from a hind leg. Dark gray markings around the eyes and nose gave the creature a strange look, too intelligent for a dog. A word came to mind — wolf, though I'd never seen one save in Kate's old books. I backed away, getting the fire between myself and the creature. Tallow hissed and retreated beneath Matthew's pack. With my free hand I drew a burning branch from the flames.

The wolf growled. For a moment I was sure it would attack. But then it shuddered, and silver light flowed over its gray fur. It shook off the light like Tallow might shake off water. Tail and teeth drew inward. Fur retreated from arms and chest and legs. The creature's eyes lost their bright wildness as it stood on two legs, leaving behind —

"Matthew?" My voice sounded far away, like someone else's voice. He was naked, shivering in the firelight, blood dripping from a ragged wound in his right calf. He stretched uncomfortably, as if uncertain how to wear his own skin.

"You —" Words stuck in my throat. Matthew ran a hand through loose hair that suddenly resembled fine fur.

He didn't seem to notice his lack of clothes. I couldn't stop noticing, though, seeing far more than I should have. Matthew looked down at his bleeding leg, then up at me. He seemed small and scared compared to the wolf he'd been.

Magic. I'd never heard of magic like this. I should have helped him. I should have offered him a blanket, cut cloth to bind his wound. I should at least have thanked him for saving my life. Yet I could only stare. How could Matthew possibly be a wolf?

Matthew looked at the knife I held, blood dripping from the blade. He reached forward, and I handed him the knife, wondering why anyone with teeth and claws would need such a weapon. My blistered fingers stung. Liquid oozed where the blisters had burst.

Matthew wiped the blood off with the blanket I'd dropped near the fire, then held the knife into the flames to cleanse it further. He reached for the blanket again and cut off several long strips of wool. He dampened the first strip with water and used it to clean the gash in his leg. The other strips he turned into bandages that he wrapped around his wound.

Matthew looked around the fire and found his clothes scattered nearby. They weren't torn, which made no sense. I turned away as he pulled on wool socks and underwear, feeling a flush crawl up my cheeks.

"Thank you, Liza." A fully clothed and booted Matthew returned my knife to me. His own knife now hung from his belt. It must have been with his clothes. He scanned the ground, picked up a strip of leather, and tied his hair back.

He looked so ordinary, just the same quiet boy I'd always known. No, not boy — I looked down at my knife as my face grew hotter. I touched my cheek and was surprised to feel dried blood there. Matthew took the cornmeal from the fire and set the pot down on the ground, limping a little as he did. Tallow crept out from her hiding place and moved closer to the flames, licking dog blood from her fur. Matthew crouched near the fire. I found myself putting distance between us once more. "How long?" I asked, my voice strange and thin.

"Two years." Matthew spoke softly but without shame.

"Ever since ..." My voice trailed off.

Matthew rubbed at his scarred wrist. "When Cam called the brambles — they grabbed me just like they grabbed Mom and Dad. I should have died with them. The thorns dug in so deep — I couldn't possibly have gotten away. Only then ..." Matthew hunched over. I looked away, into the flames.

"I didn't even understand what had happened, not right away. I just knew that I was free
and that I had to run. I didn't realize I'd
changed until later, when I was human again."
Matthew jammed both hands into his jacket
pockets. "I almost didn't remember I was human, that first time."

He wasn't a coward. He'd run because he'd
had no choice. I'd had no idea. No one had.
"You kept this hidden for two years," I said, not
sure whether hiding was the right thing to do.
Yet I'd tried to hide, too, at first.

"I didn't hide from everyone," Matthew said.

"Who knew?" There was no one I'd trust
enough to speak to of magic, not if I had a choice.

Matthew sighed and didn't answer. "The
dogs will be back, Liza. They won't be so easily
scared next time. We need to move." He stood
and began shoving gear into his pack.

I thought of his sharp claws and teeth. How
could I know he would always remember he was
human, even now? What if next time he turned
those teeth and claws on me? I didn't speak
aloud, but still Matthew glanced sharply up, as

if he'd read my thoughts. I hoped there wasn't any magic for that, or else we'd all go mad.

"Liza." He drew a deep breath. "The War is over. It's been over for almost twenty years. Magic can be controlled, no matter what your father says."

Like Cam controlled it? Like the faerie folk controlled it? "Magic kills, Matthew."

"Not always." There was real anger in those words, the first anger I'd ever heard from him. Something began building in Matthew, making the hairs on his neck stand on end. He stepped forward, lips drawing back from his teeth, fur sprouting on the backs of his hands. But before I could step back — before I could run — he clenched those hands into fists and stepped away again. He drew a deep breath and the fur receded, making him look almost human once more.

Almost. There was something in his gray eyes — too bright, too wild. Matthew looked down at his hands, then up at me, asking me without words to understand.

What I understood was that he couldn't go back home any more than I could. Neither of us could be sure we wouldn't do harm. Better to stay far from our town and those who lived there.

The dogs started howling again. I handed Matthew supplies, ignoring my stinging, blistered fingers as I did: the firewood bag and food pouch, the mug and bowl and what remained of our blanket. The pot I left behind; it was too hot to pack, and maybe the cornmeal would distract the dogs. Matthew zipped the pack closed even as Tallow leaped to my shoulders, hiding her nose in my hair.

The howls grew louder. Matthew pulled the pack over his shoulders, grabbed the torch in one hand, and quickly lit it in the fire. "Come *on*," he said, and together we fled, the howling close behind.

❧ Chapter 5 ❧

As we ran branches caught in my hair and tore at my sweater. My breath came in gasps and my back throbbed, but I kept running. Matthew limped at my side, clutching the torch. Tallow pressed up against my neck. The dogs crashed through the undergrowth and onto the trail just a few yards behind us. We veered away from them, off the path and into the forest. Yips and howls echoed close behind. I heard cracking wood and snapping bone. The barking stopped; there was a single strangled yelp and then — silence.

Matthew and I stopped running and stared at each other. Bruised purple mulberries littered the ground at our feet, filling the air with a sickly sweet scent. Mulberry trees surrounded us on all sides. The flickering circle of torchlight suddenly seemed small. Tallow mewed softly, and the branches around us bent low at the sound. I was sure their green leaves heard our every breath.

Without speaking we inched back toward the path, searching for gaps amid the trees.

The ground heaved upward. A root broke through the earth beneath my feet and I fell. Tallow leaped from my shoulders and darted into the forest. "Run!" I shouted to Matthew as I struggled to my feet, yet he stepped toward me, not away. His injured leg gave way and he fell, clutching the torch in one hand. I reached for him. Tree bark grabbed my wool sweater, pulling me back. Stickiness seeped through the sweater— blood or sap, I couldn't tell. The trees were much closer together than before.

"Liza!" Matthew rasped. He was half-buried in the dirt, roots writhing over his legs and chest and neck, face scarlet as he struggled for air. I strained toward him, but the tree behind me wouldn't let go. Bark cut through wool, biting my skin and sending fire down my back. I tried to wriggle out of my sweater, but branches snapped down from above, pinning my arms. My feet were stuck, too. I looked down and saw bark flowing like warm taffy over my boots and toward my knees. Moaning started up around us from the trees or the wind or possibly both.

Bark flowed up my thighs. I screamed as I fought the wood, calling for help — not caring that calling was useless, not caring how much my fear showed. Matthew mouthed words I couldn't hear. Pain shot through my ankles and calves. Any moment bones would snap. The torch fell from Matthew's hand and guttered out. In the sudden dimness bark rose past my waist and toward my throat, strangling my screams to whispers. From amid the trees a shadow moved toward me: a fox-sized patch of inky blackness, not tethered to any tree, darker than the moonlit night.

I heard a shout muffled through the wood around my ears. Someone ran forward, past the shadow, and placed hands against the flowing bark. "Leave be," a woman's voice said firmly. "Let blood and bone go. Seek soil, seek water, seek earth."

Bark flowed away like a receding flood. I fell forward, gasping for breath. The woman knelt beside Matthew and put her hands to the roots that held him. As she spoke those roots whipped back, flailed in the air, and withdrew into the soil. Matthew sat up, coughing violently. The metallic tang of blood mixed with the sweet smell of the mulberries. Even by moonlight, I saw the concern on the woman's pale features.

The shadow was gone.

I crawled to them. Matthew opened his mouth as if to speak, then shut his eyes and slumped forward instead. His breathing was ragged and slow; his hair fell limp over his face. His clothes were torn, covered with dirt or blood or maybe both. Dark bruises stood out against his neck. His pack was gone, leaving behind just a few scraps of nylon in the dirt.

"Can you stand?" the woman asked me, her eyes still on Matthew, her voice the same voice that had told the trees to let go. She was younger than Mom, older than me. Her long hair was pulled back in a braid.

I nodded and forced myself to my feet, back aching, ankles throbbing.

"Good," the woman said. "Once a tree has tasted blood it won't forget the taste for long. We must leave this place, and I cannot carry you both."

I reached for Matthew's hand, drew back. "Will Matthew ..." I couldn't speak the thought aloud.

"I don't know," the woman said. "I'm not a healer. We must get back to my town, where my brother can look at him." She reached for Matthew and, with more strength than I expected, lifted him over her shoulder. Matthew hung there, limp as a sack of grain.

"You never should have followed me," I whispered.

The woman started walking. I followed, ignoring pain, determined not to slow her down. The way ahead of us was clear, even though a moment earlier the trees had been so thick. Tallow appeared from somewhere in the forest and trotted along beside us as if nothing had happened.

Night sounds started: chirring crickets, a

hooting owl, a wail like a baby's cry. I glanced up, knowing we'd have no chance against an owl's talons now.

Clouds thickened over the moon and the owl fell silent. The woman seemed to have no trouble seeing in the dark. We came to a wider path and moved more quickly over the packed dirt. Pain knifed through my knee as well, and I fought not to limp.

"What possessed you to walk the woods at night?" our rescuer asked. I heard no accusation in her voice, only curiosity. She sounded so ordinary now, yet somehow she'd made the trees let us go.

"How ..."

The woman shifted Matthew's weight on her shoulder. "Trees have always listened to me, since I was a child. Who knows how such things happen? Come, faster if you can. You were lucky. I don't normally patrol quite so far. I don't know what compelled me to do so today." The moon came out again and lit her smooth, troubled face. "I only hope we're in time. I am called Karin, by the way. And you are?"

"Liza."

The night deepened around us, but the trees kept their distance. At last the path left the forest and came to a hedge, where hawthorn and ivy and briars were all woven together into a wall. Karin reached for the green leaves, and for a moment vines seemed to twine lovingly around her hands. I backed away, fearing those vines would consume us, but Karin showed no fear. "These two humans are Matthew and Liza. I ask you to grant them safe passage." She glanced down at Tallow and smiled a little. "Them and their feline companion."

The greenery rustled and parted, forming an archway. "Walk quickly," Karin said.

The hedge could have swallowed us whole. "Wait!" I looked wildly around. A shadow — the shadow I'd seen in the mulberry grove — flowed from forest to path, moving toward us.

Karin didn't seem to notice. She was already on her way through, taking Matthew with her. I had no choice — ignoring the shadow, ignoring the chill seeping into the air, I closed my eyes and plunged after her.

I heard voices on the other side and saw figures rushing forward. The pain in my back and legs turned hotter. I stumbled. Someone caught me, and all the world went dark.

❧ Chapter 6 ❧

I knelt on a moonlit hillside, sifting shards of jagged bone through my hands. I knew I didn't belong here, but still I searched, knowing there was someone, something I needed to find before I could go.

A shadow rose from the fragments. Shadow hands reached toward me, and I reached back, but then howls cut through the night.

The shadow melted into earth as a creature trotted toward me, larger than a dog, teeth gleaming. "Liza," the wolf said, and its voice was a human voice, its eyes human eyes. As the wolf met my gaze I turned away. It loped on, disappearing into the dark.

Out of the night a voice called, "Lizzy, my baby, my girl – " I stumbled to my feet and chased after the sound, knowing that if only I could catch it all would be well, night forgotten, shadows forced to flee. I ran until my legs cramped and my knees gave way. I fell then, and bark rose up to catch me. I tried to cry out, but wood clogged my throat and sealed my lips. It forced its way past skin and bone, through ears and eyes and heart —

I woke and bolted upright, screaming. Dream fragments fled like sparks from a blacksmith's forge. I was sitting on a feather mattress in a wooden frame, surrounded by white walls and dark windows. A small lamp burned on a dresser nearby. Someone had pulled off my boots, and bruises the color of mulberry juice stained my swollen feet and ankles. My sweater was covered with dried blood.

The latch clicked in the door. A woman with wild silver eyes stepped into the room, braided hair clear as glass falling down her back.

I swallowed my screams as I stared at her. Was this what my sister would have grown to, had she lived?

The woman looked back at me. "Caleb said we should expect you to wake soon."

I knew her voice. "Karin?" She'd looked so different in the dark. I hadn't realized magic was rooted in her so deeply. Yet you didn't speak to trees without magic — or if you did, the trees didn't listen. I'd been too hurt, too scared, to think it through.

"Yes, of course." Karin stepped forward and offered me a mug filled with dark liquid. "Here, this will help with the pain."

I just kept staring. She was too old to have been born with magic, like Rebecca. *Trees have always listened to me, since I was a child.* Had magic found her later, the way it had found Cam?

I hadn't known there was magic that could make a tree release its hold. Matthew had known, though. He'd said magic didn't have to kill.

"Matthew." I looked around the room. He wasn't there. I shoved the mug aside and tried to stand.

Daggers of heat stabbed through my back. My knees gave way. I reached upward, like a swimmer struggling through deep water, but darkness found me once more.

This time I dreamed only of silver light. Light flowed around me, over me. Slow at first, hesitant, then stronger, like a gathering wave. I threw my arms up against this new magic, trying to protect myself, but instead of pain or heat I felt only cool, cool healing.

*   *   *

When I woke again, Tallow lay purring on my chest.

I opened my eyes and saw a girl, maybe ten or so, red hair pulled back into a tangled ponytail. She scratched the old cat behind the ears, and Tallow bent her head this way and that in response.

"You're awake!" the girl said, then pulled her hand guiltily back. "Sorry. Dad said I should ask before I pet your cat. But you don't mind, do you?"

"Not if she doesn't." I nudged Tallow aside and sat up, expecting pain. Tallow leaped to the floor.

My back didn't hurt, and neither did anything else. I stretched, knowing I couldn't possibly have healed that fast, not unless I'd slept for weeks and weeks. The girl smiled. "I don't have a cat. I have two goats, but that's not the same thing."

I stood. The wood floor creaked beneath my feet. My legs trembled, then steadied. Still I felt no pain. Even the blisters on my fingers were gone.

"Hey, you really are better!" The girl's smile turned to a grin. "I told them so! I told them I was old enough to help, and not just with little stuff like bumped toes or scraped knees. They didn't believe me, though, not until they had no choice. Wait here — I'm supposed to tell Dad and Caleb as soon as you wake. What's your cat's name?"

"Tallow."

"Tallow's a good name. I'll be back."

I heard her footsteps clomping through the hall, then back again and down the stairs. Tallow leaped from floor to dresser, from dresser to window. She stretched out on the sill and closed her eyes, morning sun bright on her fur.

It had been night when we came here. Night when Matthew —

I went very quiet, listening. I heard a few birds outside the window as well as movement down the hall. The bruises on my ankles were gone, and someone had replaced my torn clothes with a soft wool nightgown. From downstairs I heard some-one — the girl — talking to herself as she moved about.

I left the room and crept down the hall. The floor sighed beneath my feet.

Through an open doorway I saw Matthew lying motionless in another bed, his skin dull and gray. A man bent over him. He had clear hair like Karin's, only it hung loose to his shoulders. I felt a shiver of familiarity without knowing why. A second man with ordinary reddish-brown hair stood by his side, watching him.

The first man pressed his hands to Mat-thew's bare chest. Matthew's eyes went wide. He opened his mouth as if to scream, but only a strangled whine came out. The stranger pressed harder, lips moving to words I couldn't hear, silver light flowing from his hands.

I forced myself not to cry out. Matthew arched his back, and I knew he was in pain. I reached for my knife before realizing I didn't have it. Instead I entered the room, quiet like Father had taught me, scanning the floor and dresser for something to use as a weapon.

The red-haired man looked up, and his eyes locked on mine. I froze in place as he crossed the room. "Don't," he whispered. "If you interfere with Caleb's healing you could kill them both."

Healing? That didn't look like healing. But I waited as the man gave me an apologetic smile. "I'm Samuel," he said, still whispering. "And I understand you're Liza."

I nodded, my eyes not leaving Matthew. He fell limp in the bed, eyes shut, chest moving uneasily up and down. Pale-haired Caleb collapsed into a chair, watching me through half-lidded eyes — with suspicion or curiosity, I couldn't tell.

"Come," Samuel said. "It's safe now." I went to Matthew's side, even as Samuel laid a hand on Caleb's shoulder.

Caleb looked up. "This is all I can do for now," he said. "For now, it is enough."

Matthew opened his eyes as my hand brushed his arm, then closed them again, as if that took too much work. His skin was warm. I looked to Caleb.

"His chances slowly improve," Caleb said wearily. "A few hours ago I didn't know whether he'd live through the night."

I watched the uneasy rise and fall of Matthew's chest. He, at least, could have stayed hidden, yet instead he'd followed me into the dark.

I forced myself to meet Caleb's eyes. They were silver like Karin's, bright with magic. "You saved Matthew's life."

Caleb met my steady gaze. "I cannot promise that yet. But I am doing what I can."

"With magic." My words held more of a challenge than I'd intended. I hadn't known there was magic that could heal, any more than I'd known there was magic that could force trees to release their hold.

Caleb nodded, but his expression grew more guarded. "Magic was the best tool at hand. Would you have chosen another?"

Matthew looked so small lying there, laboring with each breath. So human, no hint of wolf about him. "We are in your debt," I said, bowing my head.

Caleb nodded, but the guarded expression remained. Samuel said, "You've been here most of the night, Caleb. You need food and rest. Allie's cooking breakfast—"

"I'll be along soon," Caleb said. "I want to watch the boy a while longer."

"I'll watch," I told him.

"I'm to bring you down for breakfast, too," Samuel said. "Allie—that's my daughter—was very clear about that."

Before I could ask why a child would have any say in the matter, Caleb said, "Trust your healer, Liza. Allison may be young, but her instincts are good."

"Healer?" I asked, feeling stupid.

Caleb nodded soberly. "Matthew wasn't the only one in need of healing when Karin brought you here. I hadn't the strength for you both. We're lucky Allison was up to the task. Now go. I'll head down when you return, and you may sit with Matthew as long as you wish then."

A scowl crossed Matthew's face between breaths. I wanted to tell him everything would be all right, but I didn't know that. "I'll be back," I promised him instead, and followed Samuel down the stairs. The girl—Allie—knelt by the living room fireplace, ladling porridge into plastic bowls. My stomach rumbled at the smell.

"Liza!" She dropped the ladle, splattering porridge. Samuel laughed and handed her a towel. I remained in the doorway, uncertain. Father would have slapped me for so carelessly wasting food. Mom would have been calmer, but she wouldn't have laughed.

Allie mopped up the porridge and placed the bowls on a table near the fire. "Come on," she said. "You have to eat after a healing. That's what Caleb taught me, and it's true for healer and patient both. I'm starving. Come on!"

A bit of porridge had splattered her hair. She didn't seem to notice. Her eyes were brown, and she had a scattering of freckles over her nose. She looked perfectly ordinary, no hint of magic about her. If there were any clear strands in her hair, they were as few and as hidden as Cam's had been. How could this child have wielded the magic that healed me? I should have thanked Allie, but I felt a surge of anger instead.

Why should this town have magic that healed, while in my town magic only killed? I forced my anger down as I sat with Allie and Samuel at the table. I didn't want to seem ungrateful.

Samuel poured tea into chipped old ceramic mugs. Like at home, the mugs were covered with words from Before that no longer had meaning: *University of Missouri. St. Louis Cardinals. Disneyland.*

The porridge had a burned edge. I didn't care. I ate hungrily, tasting bits of meat mixed in. Samuel ate more slowly. "It's — very good," he managed.

"Liar," Allie said, but Samuel didn't slap her for that, either. "It's better than good, it's" — she swallowed a mouthful and sputtered — "oh," she said.

"I like it." I quickly finished my bowl, and Allie filled it again. I remembered Matthew's cornmeal boiling over onto the fire.

"You really are better, aren't you?" When I nodded, Allie turned to her father. "See? I told you I could do it."

Samuel ruffled her hair. "And you were

right, and we all should have trusted you sooner."

"Exactly." Allison gave him a smug grin, then turned to me. "How's your back? That was the worst part, you know." She shivered, and the smile left her face. "I've never seen a tree attack anyone—I can only imagine. But that's all healed, right?"

I nodded again, not telling her that not all my injuries had come from the tree. I suspected such things didn't happen in her town, either.

"So where are you from?" Samuel asked me.

I tensed. Could Kate—or, worse, Father—have warned the other towns to keep an eye out for Matthew and me, to return us home or to destroy us? But no, outsiders didn't visit our town. We turned strangers away, with words if possible, by force if need be. No one knew what danger or magic a stranger might bring.

"Wait a moment." Samuel left the room and came back with a folded sheet of smooth, thin paper from Before. The yellowing edges crumbled as he unfolded it. *St. Louis and Vicinity,* the paper said.

"A map," Samuel explained. "The blue lines are rivers. The blacks and reds are — were — roads."

The names of towns were scattered across the lines, close together in the east, farther apart in the west and south. The city of St. Louis was written larger than the others, and a thick line crossed it out. Thinner lines crossed out most of the other towns, too.

"We're here." Samuel pointed to a town west and south of St. Louis, circled in green. "Washville. And you?"

"Franklin Falls." I scanned the map. I hadn't known there were once so many towns.

Samuel found Franklin Falls before I did. It was circled in red but not crossed out. "Not far," he said. "Fifteen miles, maybe less. But red means we don't trade with you." He looked at me as if expecting some answer to that.

Allie gazed longingly at the map. "Dad says I'm too young to go Outside. But he thought I was too young to heal you, too, and he was wrong about that."

"One thing at a time," Samuel said. "Be

patient with me, Allie."

"I *hate* being patient." She took the empty
bowls from the table as her father carefully
folded up the map again. When she returned,
she said, "Come on, Liza. Time for you to get
back to bed."

"I'm okay," I said, but a loud yawn escaped
my lips. Samuel and Allie both laughed. I looked
down, heat rushing to my cheeks.

I let Allie lead me up the stairs. When she tried
to drag me toward the room where I'd wok-
en, though, I pulled firmly away and entered
Matthew's room instead. "You need sleep!" Allie
protested, following me.

Caleb stood when he saw us, gesturing me to
the chair. "He's holding steady for now."
Matthew's eyes were shut, the rise and fall of his
chest uneven, but at least he was still breathing. I
let out a breath I hadn't known I'd held.

"Caleb!" Allie said. "She should be resting.
You know she should."

Caleb crossed the room and put his hands on
Allie's shoulders. "That's a lesson you'd best
learn, then. Not all your charges will do what's

best for them, and you need to find ways to work with that."

"But how?" She looked up at Caleb. Dark shadows lay under his eyes. "You look awful! Will you at least rest?"

"Yes, Allison. I will rest. But first I must talk to Liza." He turned to me. "You will call me if you see any change in him, for good or ill, yes?"

I nodded. I didn't intend to leave Matthew's side again, not until I knew he was all right.

"Good," Caleb said. "Then there is only one matter left to discuss. Karin tells me a shadow followed you last night. A new shadow, one she's not met on patrol before. What do you know of it?"

I thought of that small inky shadow flowing toward me amid the mulberry trees and then again at the hedge. "Nothing." I didn't know where the shadow had come from or why it had followed us. Though I had seen it before, I realized with a start—in my restless dreams after Mom had left.

Caleb's eyes narrowed, but he said only, "You need not fear. The Wall kept the shadow at bay. Karin will make certain it continues to do so. But we must know what this shadow is so we can banish it or lay it to rest." Caleb's voice held a strange edge, nothing like Karin's understanding smile.

"I don't know." I shied back, fearing anger, but Caleb only frowned.

"Think on it," he said. "We dare not let this go for long."

I settled uneasily into the chair as Allie pulled Caleb from the room. Why would a shadow follow me? Had my magic somehow called it out from among the trees? I listened to Matthew's ragged breathing. Magic had saved his life.

I didn't mean to fall asleep and only knew I had when I woke to Allie draping a blanket over me. "There's a pillow on the floor," she said. "You could at least lie down."

I remained in the chair, though. Tallow padded in from the hall and jumped into my lap. I held the cat tightly, thinking this time I would stay awake. But Allie needn't have worried. Soon I slept once more.

*   *   *

When I next woke it was night, and Matthew was muttering in his sleep. "Can't," he said. "Can't let him ..." He drew shallow breaths between words. "We can't!" Matthew jerked upright, gasping in pain. I stood and moved to him, but he flung his arms out in the darkness, shoving me back. I reached forward again, but as I did Caleb was by my side, setting hands on Matthew's shoulders and easing him back to the bed.

I hadn't heard Caleb enter the room. And I'd been listening. I always listened—Father had taught me how. No one walked that quietly.

"Rest," Caleb whispered to Matthew. He reminded me of Karin, speaking to the trees. "Seek rest, seek comfort, seek sleep."

"I'll kill him," Matthew growled. "Tear him limb—from limb." His voice was hoarse, as if his throat were lined with wool.

"Be at peace," Caleb said.

Matthew's words grew softer. "I promised. Promised Cam that he—would be—the last—"

I heard footsteps down the hall. Samuel

entered the room and flipped a switch in the wall. Harsh yellow light flooded the room. I gasped aloud as Allie followed him in, rubbing her eyes.

Caleb pulled the covers down. Beneath them Matthew wore only a loose pair of trousers. Caleb's hands moved over Matthew's chest and throat, both of which were covered with bruises. Bruises and a fine layer of gray hair — wolf hair. It covered the back of Matthew's hands, too, and poked out around his ears. I hadn't noticed in the dark.

If Caleb saw, he gave no sign. "I don't like the fluid I feel in the boy's lungs. But we need to fix his ribs soon, too. Allison" — Allie moved to his side — "be my watcher. Maybe I can do both."

Caleb closed his eyes, hands moving over Matthew's skin. Silver light flowed beneath Caleb's fingers, and I fought the instinct to pull Matthew away, to rescue him from this magic instead of letting it heal him. I clenched my hands and stepped back toward the dresser instead. A bare glass ball glowed in the dresser lamp, bright as a miniature sun. I reached toward that light. The ball was hot. I jerked my hand away. Samuel moved to my side. "Got the generator running on methane two years ago," he said with a smile. "Magic can't do everything, you know."

I drew my fingers to my mouth. It felt like magic, no matter what Samuel said. Tallow leaped to the dresser, sniffed the light suspiciously, and batted at a spot in front of it.

Matthew whined softly and scratched the air. His arms began to shift, skin giving way to fur, nails turning to claws—but then they were only hands once more.

If Caleb was frightened, he gave no sign of that, either. Allie touched his elbow. "Enough," she said.

Caleb drew back with a tired sigh. "Thank you, Allison."

Samuel said to me, "Allie's been Caleb's watcher for almost a year. Ever since Caleb started teaching her."

Matthew's breathing was quieter now, more even. He sat up slowly and opened his eyes. "All right." His voice sounded weary beyond all words. "I'll stay hidden. I'll stay safe. To protect the others. But only because Tara asks it."

He turned away and buried his head against the pillow. I heard him sobbing softly.

Caleb turned to me, his question clear enough. But I couldn't answer this one, either. I didn't know whom Matthew wanted to tear apart. Didn't know if he really would have had Tara — had my mother — not asked him to hold back.

A cold feeling settled into my stomach. Mom couldn't possibly have told Matthew to hold back, not unless she'd already known he was a wolf.

As I listened to Matthew's quiet sobs, I wondered what else my mother knew — and what else she hadn't told me.

❧ Chapter 7 ❧

I slept fitfully for the rest of the night, waking whenever Matthew wheezed or coughed or turned in his sleep.

Sometime after daybreak he must have fallen silent, though, because I slept for a long time then, and woke when it was evening once more. I jerked awake with a start and saw Matthew sitting against his pillows, staring at me. Tallow slept at my feet. She'd drifted in and out of my lap all night.

"Liza." Matthew's voice was raspy, but he no longer struggled for breath. "You're all right?"

"*I'm* all right?" I didn't know whether to yell or cry. "You nearly died, and you want to know if I'm all right?"

Matthew laughed, a painful sound. "I'll take that as a yes. Where are we?"

"A town. Washville." I fought to lower my voice. Was he really going to be all right? The thought of those mulberry roots strangling the breath from him still sent cold shivers down my spine. "What do you remember?" I asked.

"Dogs," Matthew said, and his brow creased. "Trees." He hunkered deeper into the pillows. He looked so weak, so pale. His hair hung lank and tangled about his face. "Do you trust them?" he asked at last. "The people here, I mean."

They were strangers. We weren't supposed to trust strangers. Yet I did trust them — because of those strangers Matthew sat beside me, breathing without pain, far from the trees that had nearly killed us both.

Caleb knocked and entered the room. Allie trailed behind him with a pile of clothes in her arms. Caleb leaned down and ran hands over Matthew's skin, tilting his head to one side as if listening for something. "Better," he declared.

"Much better."

Matthew grasped Caleb's hands. "Thank you," he said, "for all you've done for us."

For the first time, Caleb smiled. The expression drew my gaze from his magic-touched hair and eyes, making him seem more ordinary. "You are welcome, Matthew from Franklin Falls."

Matthew sighed and released his grip. Within moments he slept once more.

Allie looked up at her teacher. "He's going to be all right, isn't he Caleb?" Her voice so clearly sought reassurance. I waited for Caleb's answer, not admitting that I sought it, too.

"One can never be certain. But yes, I believe with time he will heal fully now."

"Oh, thank goodness," Allie said. "I could hardly sleep last night. I was that worried." She handed me the pile of clothes and gestured to where my boots, belt, and knife lay beside the dresser. "You're healed enough to eat dinner with us in the Commons tonight."

I shook my head and glanced at Matthew. "I'll stay here."

"I'll stay with him," Caleb said. "The air will

do you good. I promise to send for you should his condition change."

"You've already done so much for us." Surely this town's patience, its kindness, couldn't hold forever.

The smile left Caleb's face. Suspicion returned to his eyes. "We have done what people do. Would your town have done differently, Liza?"

My town did only what it needed to survive, but shame reddened my cheeks. This town had survived, too, after all.

"Let me know when you're ready for dinner," Caleb said, "and I'll take your place in that chair." He left without looking at me again. Allie followed a moment later.

Matthew still seemed to be asleep, but I turned away from him to dress, pulling on wool underwear, sweater, and leather pants. I pulled my boots and belt over that, stopping to stare thoughtfully at my knife. They trusted me as well if they'd left me my knife. Evening sun reflected off the blade. The glare hit my eyes, so fast I couldn't turn away, and by that light I saw —

A man with clear hair and silver eyes, standing amid fire-blackened trees, ash falling like snow to his outstretched hands. A dead hawk lay at his feet, and the horizon glowed with flame —

A small inky shadow rising from a bone-covered hillside, flowing over earth and around trees, while somewhere far away a baby cried —

Mom reaching toward the surface of a huge curving mirror, clutching the metal disk she always wore and whispering a few words. Moonlight reflected off the disk, off the mirror, off the tears on her cheeks. At last the mirror parted like water, and she stepped through —

I reached after her. Someone cried out. Pain sliced through my palm, and the vision was gone. I fell to my knees, clutching the knife's blade so tightly I feared to let go. I knew there'd be pain when I did.

Another hand touched mine. Caleb unfolded my fingers from around the blade, one by one. Allie knelt beside him. As Caleb drew the knife away, she pressed a strip of yellowed sheet from Before against my hand. My palm and fingers throbbed as I watched bright red blood spread through the bandage. Allie pressed another strip over the first. Blood stained Caleb's fingers and dripped from the blade he now held. I stared at him, knew him: the young man in my visions who'd walked amid the dead trees.

He set the knife down on the dresser and put a hand on Allie's shoulder. "Do you want to heal this, or shall I?"

"She's my charge." Allie's voice shook, but her hand, pressing the bandages to mine, was steady. Matthew reached for my other hand and squeezed it hard. When had he gotten out of bed? Allie pressed the sheets harder against my palm. I flinched as pain flared through my hand. She lessened the pressure and said, "You grabbed hold of that blade so tight. Why?"

Caleb said, "Healing first. Questions later. Always." Allie nodded and touched the bandages lightly. I felt the faintest of shivers. As I watched, the bright blood darkened and dried, its metallic scent giving way to something older and mustier.

"Good. You stopped the bleeding first." Caleb's steady voice reminded me of Father's the first time he'd set a bow in my hands.

Allie unwrapped the bandages. I bit my lip as

dried blood tore away from my skin. "Sorry," Allie muttered. She ran her cool fingers over two angry red gashes, one across my palm, one along the inside of my knuckles. "It's not very deep." She shut her eyes, scrunching her face in concentration. Her fingers grew colder. Slowly she traced the first cut, and the cold seeped through my skin, numbing it. Silver light trailed from her fingers. Beneath that light my torn skin wove itself back together, stretching uncomfortably around first one wound, then the other. The cold moved deeper, chilling bone. Just when I thought I'd have to cry out, Allie drew away. Two silver lines danced over my hand, then sank beneath the skin. The cold spread out, became part of my hand, became right. I saw no blood, felt no pain. I traced my finger over two faint white lines like old scars. I remembered a dream of silver light. I looked up at Allie in wonder.

She opened her eyes and grinned. "That was fun."

"Well done," Caleb told her.

"It was easy. Liza doesn't fuss, not like the time

Jared gashed his knee."

Caleb nodded solemnly, then turned to me.
"You were lucky. If Matthew hadn't called out, if
Allison and I hadn't come—that wound could
have been far deeper. You could have cut through
to bone."

"I know," I said, avoiding his eyes.

"Such luck does not hold forever. Let's have
the source of this so we can deal with it and your
shadow both. Tell me what you saw."

I stared at my palm, wondering how he knew I
saw anything. Yet Matthew had known, too, even
though, like Caleb, he couldn't see my visions for
himself. I shivered, remembering the soft fall of
ash from a burning sky. Healing was one thing,
but visions of death and fire, visions in which
Caleb himself played some strange part? I opened
my mouth to speak, felt my throat tighten around
the words. No. I couldn't share this, neither with
strangers nor with those I knew. I feared that if I
spoke, the visions would turn real.

Caleb frowned, his eyes bright in the fading
light. "Magic and trouble have one thing in
common. Neither grows smaller if denied. We

will speak of this again soon." He turned away, helping Matthew back into bed. Allie folded up the bloodied bandages, her grin fading. I knew she wanted answers, too, but she only said, "You're still coming to dinner, aren't you?"

Caleb had set my knife on the dresser. I took it, wiped the blade carefully on a spare bandage, and slipped it into my belt. Allie frowned at that. I glanced at Matthew, hesitant to leave him alone.

Tallow emerged from beneath the bed, stretching and yawning. Caleb turned to me again, eyes narrowed. If I stayed here, he'd only ask more questions. I took the old cat in my arms and followed Allie from the room.

*   *   *

Samuel joined us downstairs. Together we stepped outside into a twilight town much like my own: dirt path, whitewashed houses, open fields. The sky was heavy with the wet dishrag smell that came before rain. Yet beyond the houses and fields I caught glimpses of a green hedge, taller than a grown man. The Commons was the largest building in town. A cracked sign above the door read

Coffee Pot Café. "That sign used to light up pink and green," Samuel told me as we stepped inside. "Tackiest thing for miles around. I sure miss the coffee, though."

A few dozen people sat in a room lit by bright lamps much like those in Samuel's house. In one corner, someone played a tarnished old flute while others listened as they ate. Mom used to play the flute, Before, but who had time for such things now? Didn't players and listeners both have work to do, in this town as much as in mine? The listeners here included a toddler with clear hair that curled about her shoulders, but no one seemed concerned, any more than they seemed concerned about Karin or Caleb.

In a kitchen beyond a rusted metal counter, Samuel, Allie, and I served ourselves bowls of fish and bean stew from a cauldron over a hearth. Allie also handed me a round green fruit, which she called an apple. I wondered why any town would risk harvesting fruit. Corn and beans were dangerous enough, and they didn't grow on trees. Unless, of course, the apple trees listened to Karin the same way mulberry trees did.

Another couple joined us at one of the room's steel-and-plastic tables. They had a girl Allie's age with them, as well as a boy a little younger. I felt everyone's eyes on me as I ate, but no one asked any more questions. For a while Allie's gaze kept straying to my knife, as if she feared she'd find me clutching steel again at any moment. Then Tallow twined around Allie's legs, and she turned her attention to offering the cat small pieces of fish. The other girl joined in. Tallow walked back and forth between them, happily licking their fingers. I bit into my apple. It tasted so sweet my teeth hurt—sweeter than tea dosed with mint, sweeter than new-harvested corn.

As we ate, Samuel and the couple, Alan and Jan, told me about their lives. Samuel's wife, Sara, had died years ago in childbirth. I was wearing her clothes and was staying in the home she and Samuel had moved into just a few weeks before the War, right after they'd gotten married.

Samuel said Sara was in the hunting party that first discovered Caleb and Karin—they were brother and sister—traveling through the woods outside Washville. They'd come all the way from the city, where Karin had been injured fighting in the War. That startled me, both because it meant Karin was older than she looked and because I didn't know anyone who'd fought in the War. Dad had a brother in the army who had likely died in the fighting, but he hardly ever talked about that.

Yet somehow Karin had survived, maybe because Caleb had healed her. Even so, Caleb and Karin had both been in pretty bad shape. At first no one but Sara had wanted to help them, because they were strangers or because of their magic, I couldn't tell. No one trusted their magic enough to leave them unguarded, either, though. I knew how my town would have solved that—with a couple of swift strokes across their throats, as Father would say—but Washville's people brought Caleb and Karin back with them instead. Over time Caleb and Karin must have earned everyone's trust, for no one questioned their presence in Washville now. Was it because she'd fought against magic that Karin had so much magic herself? But if she'd had magic since she was a child, she'd had it since before the War. I hadn't known there were any humans with magic Before. What about Caleb? Had his magic found him Before, too? Wherever Karin's magic came from, once she was well she used it to create the hedge that surrounded the town. "And a good thing for us she did," Samuel said.

"The Wall protects us," Alan explained as he rubbed Jan's shoulders.

"Lets us decide what magic to let in," Jan agreed. "And what magic to keep ..." Her words trailed off. She stood, brushing her husband's hands away.

The boy beside Allie stared into his cupped hands, gazing in wonder at a glowing stone. It shone in licheny patches, bright violet against dull gray. Allie and the other girl stared, too. My hands flew to my mouth, afraid. Stones like that had been weapons during the War.

Yet no one else seemed frightened. "I'll get Karin," Alan said, even as Jan moved to her son's side.

"Jared," she said, but his attention was on

the rock. She knelt and put an arm around his shoulders, hugging him without disturbing the stone.

I whispered, "Don't touch any stone that glows—"

"But it's his magic," Samuel said, as if I should have known, "not some trap left over from the War."

"You mean Jared made that happen?" The room seemed suddenly cold. I imagined the light overflowing Jared's stone and consuming him, just as the blackberry plant had consumed Matthew's little brother and parents.

Alan returned with Karin in tow. The pale-haired woman was smiling. Was the stone Jared held truly no danger? Karin glanced at me and nodded, but her attention was mostly on Jared. He looked up at her, his own smile stretching to the edges of his face. Jan and Alan moved to either side of their son, each laying a hand on one of his shoulders. Samuel stood, too, as did Allie and Jared's sister. Reluctantly I stood with them. Other townsfolk gathered around in a rough circle to watch.

"You know the words?" Karin asked him.

"No harm ..." Jared began, but he sounded uncertain. Karin chanted,

"Blessed are the powers that grant me magic.
I promise to use their gift well.
To help mend my world,
To help mend all words.
And should I forget to mend,
Should I refuse to mend,
Still I will remember
To do no harm."

Jared repeated the words, line by line, his voice growing older and more serious as he did. I should have been relieved—clearly he was quite safe—but instead I frowned. Did this town believe you had only to say, "I won't hurt anyone, honest," and all magic would be tamed? If it were that simple Cam wouldn't have died.

"Your first lesson," Karin told Jared, "will be in how to douse the light you've created. Come."

"Now?" Jared sounded startled.

"Now. You'll not go to bed until you learn

something of control."

Karin took the glowing stone in one hand, Jared's hand in her other. Alan gave his son's shoulder a squeeze before Karin led him away, pride clear enough on Alan's face. Jan brushed an arm across her eyes and smiled, sadly but without fear.

Samuel laughed. "So much for my generator. Within a year we'll be lighting the whole town with Jared's stones, mark my words. It's just as well—our lightbulbs wouldn't have lasted forever."

Only the girl beside Allie scowled. "It's not fair," she said. "Jared's younger than me!"

Jan drew her into a hug. "Don't be in such a rush, Kimi. Magic is quite a responsibility. You'll have time enough later."

"It's true," Allie said. "Magic's lots of work." She glanced at me, as if I proved her point. "Come on," she told the other girl. "Let's get some cornbread and see if Tallow will eat that." She dragged Kimi back toward the kitchen, Tallow trotting at their heels.

The townsfolk began talking and drifting

back to their tables. A few stopped to shake Alan's or Jan's hand first. "That's it?" I said. A few pretty words and everything was all right?

Samuel rubbed his chin and regarded me soberly. "It's different in your town, isn't it?"

That's not our fault, I screamed silently, even as Samuel went on, "We know well enough the dangers of uncontrolled magic, Liza. There's not an adult in this town who didn't lose someone to the War."

"But now the War is over and everything's perfectly safe?" I didn't even try to keep the anger from my words.

"Magic is never safe." Samuel shut his eyes a moment, opened them again. "Yes, we've lost children to magic here. Is that what you wanted me to say? But there's not a person born since the War who doesn't have some magic. What can we do but learn to control it?"

"We are *not* all born with magic." How could he think that? My hands shook, but my voice held steady. "Not in Franklin Falls." Only Matthew and I were so cursed. And Cam. And Rebecca.

"Magic is your burden," Samuel said. "Your burden and your gift."

"Not mine." He couldn't make me accept this. "Magic destroyed the world."

"Indeed," Samuel agreed. "And now it's the only tool we have to mend it."

I thought of the wondering look in Jared's eyes. Of Allie saying lightly, "That was fun!"

"So I've been meaning to ask," Samuel said slowly, "what your magic is."

I thought of my visions: fire and ash, towers falling to dust. I thought of how Cam had laughed even as the brambles destroyed him and his parents. I felt I might throw up.

"No magic." I stumbled to my feet. The Commons seemed suddenly too small, too close. I turned from Samuel's kind gaze, and I fled.

I ran through the town, not knowing where I was going, stopping only when the green Wall loomed up in front of me. I fell to my knees there. Green tendrils stretched out to twine around my fingers. I jerked back, skin prickling. Magic like this had killed in my town. Yet Karin had built the Wall on purpose, for protection.

Thunder rumbled somewhere far away. "Rebecca," I whispered. I tried to picture Father taking my sister in his arms, asking her to repeat a few words, speaking to her of magic with the same gentleness he'd used when teaching me to hunt and plant corn. The vision wouldn't hold. I remembered instead cracked bones and a moonlit hillside. "Rebecca." I imagined my sister on the other side of the Wall, asking me without words for safe passage. I whispered her name again, reached toward her, drew back. Rebecca was gone. I knew that. There was no use in pretending.

I was crying, not sure when I'd started, staring up at the Wall and at clouds lit by moonlight from below. Yet I was listening, too, so when I heard footsteps, I brushed my tears away and looked up.

Two small figures approached the Wall, several yards away. They didn't seem to notice me.

"Come on," a girl said in the sort of worried whisper that always carries. Kimi, who had been angry about her brother's magic. "You're the one who always said you wanted to see

Outside."

"I do." Allie's voice, fiercer and quieter. "But not now. Not until the healing's through."

"The stranger is fine. Even I can see that. Come *on*."

Allie drew her arms around herself. "You don't understand. Maybe when your magic — "

"Magic!" Kimi shouted. "I am so tired of hearing about magic!" She whirled away from Allie and darted through the hedge. Vines and branches parted, letting her go.

"Kimi, no!" Allie ran after her and the Wall let her through as well. Maybe the Wall cared only whom it let in, not out, or maybe it already knew Allie and Kimi. Or maybe it was magic and didn't much care who died. I scrambled to my feet, pushing thoughts of Rebecca aside, knowing I needed to drag Kimi and Allie back before they got hurt.

As I stood I heard a scream beyond the Wall. I plunged forward, barely noticing as the vines parted to let me through.

~ Chapter 8 ~

"What'd you have to touch it for?" Allie yelled. I ran toward her voice.

Kimi lay on the ground, shivering violently. Allie ran hands over Kimi's arms, legs, chest. A few yards away, a small dark shadow lay puddled beneath the moonlit clouds, the same shadow that had followed us from the mulberry trees. Without knowing why, I reached for it. The shadow rose and surged toward me. I jerked my hands back.

"Go away!" I shouted in panic. "Go *away.*"

The shadow flowed swiftly back, disappearing among the trees. I thought I heard a low wail, then there was no sound save for Kimi's chattering voice.

"It was just a shadow!" Kimi whimpered, as if she didn't know the danger shadows could hold. I knelt by her side.

Allie looked up. Relief flooded her features, as if somehow I could make everything all right.

I rubbed Kimi's hands, trying to get warmth into her, and realized those hands weren't even cold. Yet she kept shivering.

"Not f-f-f-fair," Kimi chattered. "Didn't kn-n-n-n-ow!"

"Know what?"

"The shadow," Allie said. "I tried to warn Kimi it was magic, but she didn't listen. She couldn't feel it the way I could, because she doesn't have her own magic yet. So she touched it. Put her hand right through." Allie scowled, but she looked more scared than when she'd seen me clutching my knife.

"Thought you were making it up," Kimi said. "Ab-b-b-out the magic. But it was so c-c-c-cold."

I helped Kimi to her feet, guilt washing over me. That shadow wanted me — had followed me. When I reached a hand out, it was drawn to me.

Kimi shivered harder. "Come on," I said, urging her back toward the Wall. Allie moved to the girl's other side even as Kimi stumbled. Kimi fell to her knees and hunched over, rocking back and forth, refusing to stand when Allie tugged her arm. I picked up the girl instead, staggering a little under her weight, and carried her to the Wall. Vines and branches parted for us once more.

Alan met us on the other side, panting as if he'd been running. He took his daughter from my arms. Samuel was there, too. Allie ran to him, sobbing. "Don't blame Kimi, she didn't know, it's not her fault—"

Samuel drew her close. "You're all right?" he said.

"Yes, I'm fine, but Kimi—"

"Get Caleb," Samuel told her. "We'll discuss blame later." As Allie ran for help, he shook his head. "I told her she wasn't allowed Outside." He seemed more scared than angry. Alan rocked his daughter, telling her over and over again that everything was all right, even though he couldn't possibly know that. Allie returned several paces behind Caleb, who strode to Alan's side. Caleb took Kimi in his arms and lowered her to the ground while Alan looked on anxiously. The girl's eyes were squeezed shut, and she'd drawn her arms around herself as if for warmth. Caleb slowly moved his hands from her head to her toes, his own expression unreadable.

"I tried to heal her," Allie said, kneeling beside him. Panic edged her words. "I tried, but I couldn't find what was wrong!"

"That's because this isn't a matter of skin or blood or bone," Caleb said soberly. "It's on the level of essence. Soul, you might say."

Allie swallowed. "That sounds bad."

"Not so bad as it could be. Just ... tricky to find. Here, I'll show you." He laid one hand over Kimi's head, the other over her heart. Allie placed her small hands on top of his large ones. They both closed their eyes. Silver light bloomed beneath Caleb's palms.

"Oh!" Allie said. "But that's easy! Why didn't I see?"

The light sank down and disappeared. Kimi stopped shivering and opened her eyes. Alan knelt beside her; she threw her arms around his neck, clinging hard, as if seeking warmth still.

"Stay with her tonight," Caleb said. "Keep her warm. Send for me if anything happens. I don't care how late. You know that."

"I know, and — thank you." Alan glanced at me. "And thank you, too, for bringing her home." He carried his daughter away, holding her as if she were a much younger child.

Caleb looked at Allie and me. He drew his hands together and rested his forehead on them. "You'd best tell me exactly what happened."

I looked down, ashamed, leaving Allie to tell the story.

"I didn't know what to do," she said at last. "If Liza hadn't come ..." The words trailed off.

"You did well," Caleb assured her. He turned to Samuel. "Take her home. She's had a long couple of days."

Allie started to protest, but at a glance from Samuel merely sighed. "Are you coming, too, Liza?"

"Liza will be along shortly." The ice in Caleb's voice startled me.

Allie didn't seem to notice. "Well, hurry up.

I'm still Liza's healer, you know. And she needs rest."

Caleb watched Allie follow her father away. "Kimberly was lucky. Allison, too. If either of them had touched the shadow for longer, it could have done them real harm. I'll allow many things, Liza, but I will not allow you to endanger the children of this town." His eyes reminded me of frost before dawn. I backed away a little. "There are many shadows left over from the War," Caleb said. "Tell me the nature of your magic and how this shadow came to be bound to you."

"I don't know."

"You will tell me. Now." Caleb grabbed my arm, drew a small mirror from his pocket, and held it before me. I tried to turn away, but moonlight shone through the clouds and reflected off the glass. The light burned, cold as a healer's touch. I screamed, and as I screamed I saw —

A huge metal arch stretching from river to sky and back again. A dark-haired young woman, her face streaked with tears, walking toward the arch's base, closer and closer until it towered above her like a giant curving mirror. She walked on, stepped through the mirror's bright surface, and disappeared.

I heard an indrawn breath and knew I wasn't alone. Somehow Caleb had followed me into this vision. I fled from him, and as I fled I saw —

Towering oaks and maples stretching branches down toward the earth. Shadows bridged the gaps between leaf and land, and the earth shuddered at their touch. Trenches gaped open, filled with metal and bone.

I flinched away, but Caleb grabbed my shoulder, forcing me to look — to see the dark fluid that stained the bones, to taste the metallic tang at the back of my throat.

I shut my eyes, and behind closed lids I saw —

Darkness. Cool, silent darkness, save for the tread of footsteps on a wooden floor. A shadowy figure carried a bundle in his arms. My father. The bundle began to cry, and from down the hall my mother whimpered in her sleep, but I only watched, doing nothing. Father descended the stairs, leaving darkness behind him. I turned from that darkness, and as I turned I saw —

A woman kneeling by a lake. Sun lit the blackened stubs of trees around her. Dark cinders coated the earth. Only the lake glowed red, fire dancing beneath the water, light reflecting off the woman's face —

My mother's face. "Liza," Mom whispered, but she looked at the water, not me. "I was a fool, Liza. Leaving for a memory, a dream, a hope that should have died long ago."

Caleb's fingers dug into my shoulder, holding me, hurting me.

"Hope has no place after the War. I should have remembered that." Fire lit Mom's features, tear-tracks drying on her cheeks.

Something was wrong, more wrong than my mother's tears, more wrong than the dead trees and burning water —

"Lizzy," Mom said, and the ache in her voice twisted knots in my stomach. "Forgive me, Lizzy."

"Mom." I reached toward her, and glass parted at my touch. I felt hot wind against my fingers. Caleb's grip tightened as the sense of wrongness thickened, like soup left too long on the fire. I reached for Mom's face, but she was too far away.

Mom leaned nearer to the burning water, hair trailing so close I thought it would catch fire. "Kaylen?" she whispered, then shook her head as if at some foolish thought. *"So much time. So much grief—"*

I reached for Mom again, aching to take her out of that place and bring her home. But flames rose from the water, hiding her, consuming her. In those flames I saw—

A girl falling to the floor, crying out as her knees hit hard tile. A man towered over her, raising his belt. "Weak," the man hissed. "You're weak, Liza." Father's belt fell, breaking skin. I bit my lip to keep from crying out, drew my arms over my head against more blows—

They didn't come. I heard shattering glass and a voice softly calling my name. I looked up into silver eyes.

Not Caleb's eyes. Caleb stood nearby, hands clenched, gaze drawn inward. Karin knelt before me, a broken mirror by her side. "You're a fool," she whispered to Caleb as she helped me sit up. My neck was stiff—I'd been huddled down, just like in my vision. I gasped for breath but couldn't seem to get enough air. Splatters of cold rain fell on my face.

Karin took my hands in her own, her cool grip surprisingly strong. "Breathe slow," she said.

"Breathe deep. You can breathe. You just need to remember how. There you go. Now speak if you can. Give me some sign you've returned, and don't wander in visions still."

I ran my tongue over my lips, tasted blood. I looked at Caleb. He looked back, his eyes bright mirrors that saw past skin and bone. Shame tightened my stomach. He'd seen. No one had ever seen when Father — no one. Not Kate, not Matthew, not even Mom.

"I did not know," Caleb said stiffly, "that you were Tara's daughter." How did he know my mother's name? I looked down but felt him watching me still. "We need to talk," Caleb said.

"Let me," Karin said. "You will talk to me, Liza, yes?" I didn't trust myself to speak. If I spoke I would scream, or weep like a child. Yet I feared they wouldn't let me go at all if I didn't speak to someone, so I nodded.

"But she is — " Caleb began.

"Kaylen," Karin interrupted, "you told me once that preserving the present is more important than redeeming the past. I hold to that now. Go."

"I did what needed doing. And I hold to that."

"That's War talk," Karin said, her voice cold.

"You get to the root of Liza's shadow, then, before it touches any more of our children." I watched Caleb retreat. My cheeks burned.

"We will not rush this," Karin said to me. She settled cross-legged onto the grass beside me. "Magic has its own rhythms and cannot be forced. Caleb should have remembered that."

My heart pounded, as if any moment I might need to run. Raindrops trickled down my neck. I shivered and looked up at Karin. With her braid pulled back from her smooth face she looked far too young to have fought in the War.

"If you wish to tell me what you saw, I will listen," Karin said. "Visions hold less power when put into words. But I won't make you speak. And you need not tell anything you don't want to."

Trees, fire, shadow — I feared speaking would give my visions more power, not less. "I can leave," I told Karin. "If the shadow is bound to me, I can draw it away."

"You'll go nowhere," Karin said. "Not at my urging. Whatever threatens you, if we can have it out, we can deal with it. There's no magic so terrible it cannot be laid to rest."

The light rain stopped. Wind blew against my damp skin. "Ask Caleb. He saw everything. He was there."

"I'm asking you. They're your visions. Only yours. Please trust me, Liza. Not for my sake, not for Caleb's, but for your own."

Father said strangers couldn't be trusted, that trust was a child's tale swept away by the War.

"You called me," Karin said. "When the trees attacked. You called, and I came. I don't know why, but put some trust in that, if in nothing else."

The moon slipped deeper into cloud, turning Karin's face to shadow — all but her eyes, which remained bright as she watched me. I took a deep breath, like when I dove beneath the surface of the river. "I saw my mother," I said.

Karin nodded, waiting. My voice grew low as the wind. "Mom told me she'd been a fool.

She asked me to forgive her, for what I don't know. She told me—but she's dead. No one ventures out alone into the night and lives."

"You did," Karin said.

"I wasn't alone." Without Matthew I would have drowned in the river or been devoured by the dogs. And Karin had saved us from the trees.

"Perhaps your mother found help, too."

I shook my head. "She was alone."

Forgive me, Lizzy. She was gone beyond anyone's forgiveness. Yet I heard myself ask, "Can visions be trusted?"

"Trusted how?"

"Are they real? Are they true? Can magic be trusted?"

"Magic can never be trusted," Karin said. "Just ask Jared, who burned his fingers more than once this evening as he learned to control his light. But as for whether you see truly—that I cannot say. Even Before visions were never simple. They're often tied up with other magic. What of the other children in your town? Do any of them have visions, and are those visions true?"

"The others have no magic," I told her, just as I'd told Samuel.

I couldn't tell whether she believed me or not. She laced her fingers together, rested her chin on them, and asked, "Could you tell where your mother was in your visions? That might help."

Did I dare to hope? *Hope has no place after the War,* Mom had said. Yet I so wanted to believe she lived. "She was in a place of—of ash and dead trees." I should have found the memory of those blackened trunks comforting, but it only brought an acrid taste to the back of my throat. Crops wouldn't grow in so dead a place. People would die there, too. "What could kill so many trees?"

"Pray you never have to know," Karin said. "Tell me what else you saw."

I told her in bits and pieces, fragments that couldn't have made any sense. I told her what I'd seen, in this vision and in the others. A metal arch, bright as a mirror. A young woman and my mother, both stepping through the surface of that arch. Grasping trees whose shadows brought tall buildings down.

Tallow trotted to my side, a feather dangling from her mouth. I petted the cat as I continued to talk.

"Why Caleb?" I asked Karin. Caleb had been in my visions before. I dug my fingers into the damp dirt. Even the memory of how he'd invaded my thoughts made me want to crawl out of my skin.

"Time and space are fluid in visions," Karin said, but for a moment she looked very troubled indeed.

I spoke on, telling how I'd reached through Caleb's mirror and felt the wind of a dead land against my skin. The only thing I didn't share were my visions of Father. That shame belonged to — ought to have belonged to — no one but me.

At last I fell silent. A weed curled around the toe of Karin's boot, and she absently nudged it away.

"Are my visions true?" I asked again. I felt strange and calm, not how I expected to feel after speaking those visions aloud.

"I don't know."

"Might they be true?"

"They might."

And my mother might be alive. My hands clenched. "I have to find her." I couldn't do anything else, not while there might still be a chance.

Karin slowly unlaced her fingers and set her hands in her lap. "If your visions speak true, it sounds as if your mother is beyond the Arch."

How could anything exist beyond the surface of a mirror? I remembered how my hand had moved through Caleb's smaller mirror, though. "Beyond the Arch—you mean in the land of dead trees?"

Karin's gaze drew inward, as if she saw something I couldn't. "That would be Faerie," she said.

A few cold raindrops slid beneath my sweater. Why would even faerie folk live in such a place? It was living trees they'd called against us, after all. "I have to go there," I said, even as I wondered what chance I could possibly stand against faerie folk. Yet the land had been empty in my visions. Perhaps the faerie folk didn't live there anymore, either.

"I'll train you first," Karin said. "You'll need all the magic you have to survive beyond the Wall—and in Faerie."

I shook my head as I remembered the dogs and the mulberry trees and a night Matthew and I almost hadn't survived. *So much time,* Mom had said, but I had a feeling there was hardly any time at all. Something was wrong—I knew that now as surely as I had known it in my vision. Something was wrong, and it already might be too late to set things right. "I need to go now."

Karin frowned and reached for the Wall, as if touching wild things helped her think better. Ivy curled like a bracelet around her wrist, and a few stray shoots wove themselves into her sleeve. "I would go with you, but I must stay here to maintain the Wall. Caleb will go, if you ask."

"No!" The thought of traveling with Caleb after all he'd seen, after all he'd forced me to see ... "No."

"Wait until Matthew is healed, then."

I hesitated. Matthew and I had gotten this far together, and the thought of his company was more comforting than I expected. But I remembered his ragged breathing and his pale, bruised skin. I couldn't put him in danger again. I shook my head once more. "He'll be safe here."

Karin could train him if she wanted, once he was well.

"You don't want to take this journey alone, Liza."

I said nothing. Drizzle started up again. The ivy drew back from Karin's skin and stretched toward the rain. Other vines and briars did the same, until the whole Wall reached for the sky.

Karin frowned. "It is possible," she said slowly, "that the way through the Arch was left open after the War. In that case once you reach it you need only to step through. But otherwise, if the way isn't open—then, Liza, you'll have to rely on your own magic. Your visions have power enough to let you through the Arch, just as they let your hand through Caleb's mirror. But if you fail, you could wander in visions forever. I'd rather you let me teach you."

I drew my arms around myself. "How far is the Arch? Do you know how to get there?"

Wind blew a few clear strands from Karin's braid. She was silent so long I thought perhaps she'd decided not to tell me, but then she sighed, a sound like trees in the rain. "It has been many years since I made that journey, but Samuel can show you the way on his map. I'm not sure how long it will take you—a week, perhaps. You will at least wait until sunrise to go, yes?"

"I'll leave at dawn," I agreed.

Karin nodded slowly. "Come, then. You need rest before you go."

I let her lead me back to Samuel's house. As we walked I asked, "What about the shadow? Caleb said—"

"Do not trouble yourself with what Caleb said. You have other things to think about now. I will do what I can to see that the shadow follows you no further."

Allie ran to us as Karin opened Samuel's door. The girl's wool nightgown trailed behind her. In places her loose red hair stood on end, as if she'd been running her hands through it. "What's going on?" she demanded. "Caleb said you might be leaving, but he wouldn't say why."

My chest tightened, remembering all that Caleb had seen. Only Karin's steady hand on my shoulder kept me from running away.

"He wouldn't tell me *anything*," Allie complained. "He just went up to Matthew and shut the door, wouldn't even let me in."

My stomach clenched. I shoved past Allie and ran for the stairs, taking them two at a time. Caleb had said he couldn't be certain Matthew would heal fully, even now. I threw open the bedroom door and ran to Matthew's side.

Matthew slept, quiet as a child. The tension had left his face. He breathed softly and without pain. I reached for his hand, then drew awkwardly back. He was fine.

"He'll be well enough to travel come morning." It was Caleb's voice, low and weak. I looked up and saw Caleb slumped in the chair. His face was gray, his eyes shadowed. He met my gaze, and we both flinched away. Allie ran to Caleb's side and placed her hands over his. "You pushed too hard!" she said, as if scolding a child. "You always tell me not to push too hard!"

Caleb didn't seem to hear. His hands beneath hers were clenched into fists. He looked at me again, and I looked to the floor.

"You can't go after her alone, and I know better than to expect you'd let me go with you. But the boy will go. I don't know what you are to each other, but he has followed you this far. He'll not abandon you now."

I took a step back. "How do you know I'm going?" I hadn't told anyone but Karin yet.

"It was a guess, nothing more, given what I saw. Did I guess wrong?"

He had no right to see all he did. He had no right to guess at what I'd do before I'd even decided for myself.

I heard quiet conversation and footsteps on the stairs. Samuel and Karin stepped into the room as Caleb stood, shaking, and walked toward me. My chest pounded with the fear that he might enter my thoughts once more, but he only opened his fist and dropped something into my palm — a metal disk not much wider than my thumb, hanging from a chain. "Find your mother, Liza." Caleb's voice trembled like water beneath wind. "And when you do, tell her I am sorry. Tell her she was right."

He fell to his knees. Allie cried out. Samuel and Karin ran to help him to his feet. "You need rest," Allie said severely.

Caleb stumbled toward the door. Allie started after him, but Karin laid a hand on her shoulder. "I'll see him safely home," Karin said. "He'll be fine, I promise. You stay here and help Liza pack, all right?" Allie swallowed and nodded. Karin helped Caleb from the room. "You're a fool," she said to him again, not with anger this time. Allie whispered, "Caleb could have killed himself, pushing so far without a watcher. Why didn't he call me? I would have helped him. He knows that."

Samuel drew her close. If he was still angry at her for going beyond the Wall, he gave no sign. "Caleb knew you would have stopped him. And he knew he needed to do it anyway."

"I don't *understand*," Allie complained.

I looked down at the disk in my hand. The surface was worn and tarnished, but I could tell the metalwork came from Before. The picture etched on its surface was more intricate than anything we had craft for now: on one side a man's face, on the other a silver arch over a river, stretching from one forest to another. A boat lay on the river, but the arch was what caught my eye. *A huge metal arch stretching from river to sky ...*

Words were inscribed on the disk: *Missouri* on one side, *United States of America* on the other. Old words, words from Before. But the Arch—what was it doing on the disk Caleb had handed me? That made no more sense than his knowing my mother's name. I felt like Allie, like I didn't understand. I slipped the chain around my neck, letting the disk hang beneath my sweater.

"Liza."

I looked up at the sound of Samuel's voice.

"Karin has told me where you must go, though she didn't have time to tell me why. I don't like it, but—whatever you require for your journey, I will see that you have it."

"Why?" I asked before I could stop myself. I was just a stranger here, and yet they'd done so much for me already. "Why did you let me into your town at all?"

"Because that's what people do," Samuel

said, just as Caleb had. But then he added, more softly, "Because it's what we forgot to do during the War." He stroked his daughter's tangled hair. "Because some of us have sworn, on our very lives, that we won't forget again."

ᴤ Chapter 9 ᴥ

Samuel gave me all I asked for: flint and steel, plastic water bottles, a change of clothes. Bedrolls and warm leather jackets. Several days' food.

He gave me things I didn't ask for, too, not because I didn't need them, but because I feared to ask too much: long cloaks oiled against the rain. A leather tarp, oiled as well. Cooking pots and extra socks. A hunting bow, so strong and light I knew it came from Before. A small plastic torch, also from Before, that produced a beam of cold white light at the push of a button. Tallow sniffed each item Samuel handed me as I packed. Allie watched us, sulking, from the couch.

"Most of our batteries are long dead," Samuel

said as he showed me how the torch worked. "But a few have held their charge, against all reason." He thrust the torch into my hand, along with an extra set of batteries. "I've been saving these until there was need. And I'll sleep better knowing you have a reliable light with you."

"At least tell me where you're going!" Allie said. I realized neither Samuel nor I had told her. I drew Caleb's disk from beneath my sweater and showed her the Arch.

Samuel set down the coil of rope he was handing me, good nylon rope from Before. "The Arch was where the War began. The Arch and the Needle and the Pools. You know that, don't you?"

I shook my head. I hadn't known. "The Arch was at the heart of the city," Samuel said. "St. Louis, gateway to the west. You sure you have to go there, Liza?"

The dark look on his face sent icy shivers down my spine. I knew about the city, of course, knew that it had fallen much harder than the towns. I forced my voice to stay steady, feigning confidence I didn't feel. "Karin said you know the way."

Samuel rested his head in his hands. "I know." He sounded suddenly tired. "I could still give you driving directions, right down to which interstate exit to take."

"Will you tell me?"

He said nothing.

"My mother's there. I have no choice."

"If she is there ..." Samuel frowned. "She probably didn't survive the journey, Liza. And if somehow she did survive, she wouldn't want you to follow her. She'd want you to stay safe."

I shook my head. "I can't leave her." Tallow shoved her head under my hand. I scratched the cat behind the ears. "Please. If there's something I can do for you in turn — "

"All right," Samuel said, but he kept frowning. "Hang on. I'll show you."

He left the room. Allie leaped from the couch the moment he was gone. "You can't go, Liza! You can't go somewhere so dangerous that even Dad is scared." When I gave no reply she shook her head, hair falling into her face. I saw a few clear strands scattered amid the red. "I can forbid you to go. As your healer. Just like I would forbid someone who broke their leg to walk on it." She drew a gulping breath, voice wavering between anger and tears. "At least let me see your hand. To make sure it's healing right, before you leave."

I held out my palm. The scars were barely visible now. Allie closed her eyes and ran her fingers over the two pale lines. Rain fell gently against the roof. "No sign of infection. That's good." She opened her eyes. "But you still haven't told me why you did it. Why you cut yourself like that."

"I didn't do it on purpose." I felt for the knife in its sheath. What if I didn't have someone to pull my fingers away from the blade the next time my magic led me to grab it?

Allie caught her breath as my fingers tightened around the hilt. "Don't," she said.

"I wasn't." Silently I let my hand drop.

"Promise you *won't*. Not here, and not after you leave, either. Words have power, that's what Caleb and Karin say. Especially for people with magic. It's like the oath about doing no harm. You can't say it if you don't mean it.

Promise you won't hurt yourself again."

I hadn't meant to hurt myself the first time. I didn't know where my magic would lead or what harm it might do. "I won't do it on purpose," I said.

Allie irritably brushed her hair out of her face, as if that wasn't good enough for her. "Why do you make everything so hard?" she demanded. "Why did I have to wind up with you, of all the people who could fall under my charge?"

"You healed me well," I assured her.

"No, I didn't. Because you wouldn't be afraid to promise if I had."

Samuel returned and spread his map out on the table. I knelt beside him. "We're here," he said, pointing to Washville. "If you take the main way out of town, it will eventually bring you to what's left of I-forty-four."

He took an old pencil and began tracing a route east and north. If all went well, that route would take me all the way to the Arch—and to a thick river labeled the Mississippi.

"So far," Allie breathed. Not with anger, not

with fear, but with envy.

"It would have taken only an hour or so by car," Samuel said. "On foot—I don't know. Four days, maybe? Five? It depends on the road and the trees and who knows what else." His frown deepened. "If you were my daughter, I wouldn't let you go."

"If she were your daughter, she'd never have left home at all," Allie said morosely.

Samuel refolded the map and handed it to me.

"Thank you," I said. "I'll bring it back if I can."

"You'd better!" Allie said. "You're still my charge, you know. Leaving doesn't change that." She grabbed Tallow from where the cat was trying to nose her way into my pack. Tallow squirmed, but Allie didn't let her go.

The pack was made of strong nylon, like the rope. It bulged with supplies. So did a second pack beside it, for Matthew. I still hoped to leave him safely behind, though. I'd been careful to make sure my own pack held a fair share of everything I needed.

I wedged the map into a pocket of that pack

and turned to Samuel. "Thank you. For every-thing."

He reached out and drew me into his arms, as if I were as young as Allie. I stiffened, but Samuel didn't let go. "I pray that I'm wrong, child. I pray that you find her."

*   *   *

I hadn't intended to sleep. I'd intended to lie on the couch until Samuel and Allie went upstairs, then quietly leave before Matthew could follow me. But I must have drifted off, for I woke to Matthew gently shaking my shoulder. I jerked to my feet. Matthew stood in front of me, fully dressed, his hair pulled neatly back from his face. His breathing was easy, his eyes bright and alert. He favored his left leg a little but otherwise seemed well.

Too well to risk his life all over again. "You needn't come," I said.

He ran a hand over his hair, making it pull loose around his ears, as if he were just the quiet, smiling boy who'd come to say Father was looking for me. Who'd offered to face Father with me. "I'm going with you, Liza. So there's no point in arguing, unless you want to waste time."

"Do you even know where we're headed?"

"I assume you'll tell me on the way."

Samuel came from the kitchen and handed us slices of brown bread thick with butter. Someone knocked at the door. I feared I'd find Caleb there and was relieved to see only Karin.

She smiled and took my hands. "There's no use telling you to be careful, Liza. You know that well enough. I'd offer warnings about Faerie, but I haven't been there since the War. I do not know what you'll find.

"Listen to your magic. That's the first thing I tell the children here. Don't fear it—but don't expect it to be safe, either. Don't expect it to be one thing or another at all. Magic is never simple. And it flows in both directions: a shape-shifter can return to human form, a healer can wound with her touch. Because I can draw trees to me, I can also push them away."

I felt Caleb's metal disk beneath my sweater. *Tell your mother she was right.* Right about what? "Karin, how does Caleb know my mom?"

Karin's smile turned sadder. "I think that story is not mine to tell. Ask your mother when you find her."

Matthew and I shouldered our packs. Outside, dawn was brightening to orange and light shone through scattered clouds. Karin and Samuel walked us to the Wall along a path made damp by last night's rain. Allie was nowhere in sight. I wondered if she was still angry at me for failing to make promises I didn't know I could keep.

Tallow was missing, too. I longed for her weight on my shoulders but said nothing. If I couldn't keep Matthew safe, at least I could protect Tallow. Allie would care for her well enough. She'd probably let the cat sleep on feather beds all she wanted.

At the Wall we stopped a moment more. Karin looked at me. She looked away before I could drop my gaze. "Stay to the path, don't travel at night if you can help it, and return when you can."

"Let us know that you're safe," Samuel said.

I nodded, not promising, not refusing to promise. I turned from them and stepped through the Wall's parting branches.

A moment later Matthew emerged beside me. The dirt path continued beneath our feet, just as it did on the map, so we walked on. Matthew limped a little, but he matched my pace easily enough.

If any shadow followed us, the morning was too bright for us to see it. I took off my jacket and tied it around my waist. Forest soon surrounded us, tall oaks and hickory, but the path beneath our feet remained clear, with only bits of black rock poking through here and there. Blackberry and wild plum kept to the undergrowth. Ragweed and wild grape held close to the trees.

Beside me Matthew said, "Now, Liza, where exactly are we headed?" I looked at his face, pale as if after long illness, at the way his fair hair fell around his ears. He rubbed at his scarred wrist. That and his limp seemed to be the only things Caleb hadn't healed.

I should have felt uncomfortable, alone with Matthew on the path, but I realized I was glad of his company, for all that I'd have been gladder if he'd stayed safe. One of the oaks threw an acorn at us. It grazed my ear. "We're going to find my mother, like Karin said." I picked up the acorn and flung it back into the forest.

"Good." Matthew nodded, as if finding my mom made perfect sense, as if he wanted to find her, too. "Did you see Tara? Did your magic ... show her to you somehow?"

"Is it really so clear?" I hadn't told anyone but Karin about my magic, but everyone else seemed to have figured it out on their own.

"I'm not stupid, Liza. I saw you grab at hot metal, at a knife's blade. Anyone could tell you saw something. And it's not as if you're the first person I've known with magic."

He'd said that before. I'd assumed he meant his brother, or maybe Rebecca. But Samuel said all children had magic, and in his sleep Matthew had talked about protecting the others. "Who else?" I demanded. If anyone else in my town had magic, I'd have known, wouldn't I?

The wind picked up, carrying the scent of rain. "I made a promise," Matthew said uneasily. "But perhaps one day I'll be released from it."

I'll stay hidden. I'll stay safe. But only because Tara asks it. "A promise to my mom," I said flatly.

Matthew ducked his head, and I knew I was right. The clouds thickened. I pulled on my jacket again. How much did my mother know? How much had she kept hidden? Did she trust Matthew more than me?

A butterfly flew across the road. Matthew held out his hand and it landed there. He stared at the iridescent wings as if debating whether to speak. "Before Tara left, she spoke to Gram. I didn't hear all of it. But Gram told her not to be stupid. Gram said there was nothing left for her to find. She said Tara wouldn't be welcome, even if there was. I don't know what Gram meant. You're not the only one they keep secrets from, Liza." Matthew shrugged awkwardly and changed the subject. "The things you didn't see in the cooking pot and the knife. Did they tell you where Tara is?"

Smoke rose from the butterfly's wings. I drew out Caleb's disk and pointed. "She's beyond this

Arch. In Faerie."

The butterfly burst into flame, as butterflies often did. Matthew shook warm ash from his fingers. "Well, then, we'd better get walking," he said, as if going to Faerie held no more danger than heading down to the river for water.

As we walked on, the clouds closed in and the sun disappeared behind puffs of charcoal. Matthew and I drew the cloaks from our packs. By midday rain began to fall, lightly at first, then harder.

Lightning flashed. A maple stretched toward the light. Thunder rumbled. Another flash of light. This time the bolt met one of the maple's branches. The tree seemed to draw the lightning into itself and to stand taller than the trees around it. Matthew and I ducked against the boom that followed, then walked faster, hunched against the rain and growing wind. Mud pulled at my boots. Water trickled in around the edges of my cloak.

A bluff rose to the west. Oaks and maples and elms all reached toward the rain, sighing happily as water soaked through their leaves and into their roots. The rain continued into late afternoon, then gave way to cold drizzle. The wind let up. I heard sounds that the wind and rain had hidden: the scrabbling of claws, the scream of some small rodent, low wails like a baby's cries.

Footsteps on the path behind us, squishing in the mud.

I slowed my pace and quieted my steps, listening. Matthew sniffed the air. The clouds grew thick around us, the road dark. It was still afternoon, but I couldn't tell how late. *Don't venture out alone into the dark.*

"We should make camp," I said.

Matthew nodded so quickly I knew he'd had the same thought. Whatever followed us, we'd do better with a fire at our feet and solid stone at our backs. We found a spot at the base of the bluff where the dirt road widened into a broad flat space. I set the tarp up against the bluff, fitting together the hollow metal poles Samuel had provided. Matthew gathered what dead wood he could find near the road, and beneath the shelter we coaxed a small fire from the dry undersides of the fuel. All the while the footsteps drew nearer and the sky grew darker. I untied the bow from my pack, stepped out from beneath the tarp, and nocked an arrow. Matthew moved to my side, his eyes flashing with each distant flicker of lightning.

A figure rounded the corner, cloak splattered with mud, a bundle wrapped in her arms. I drew the arrow back, then caught my breath as the figure looked up, lightning illuminating her features.

"No," I whispered. She was supposed to be safe. Safe with Samuel and Caleb and Karin. Safe behind the Wall that her town had built to protect its children.

I set the bow aside as Allie stepped into the light of our fire. The bundle squirmed. Two damp ears poked out from beneath oiled leather. Allie reached out, handing the bundle to me.

"You forgot your cat," she said.

❧ Chapter 10 ❧

Tallow climbed into my arms and licked my nose once, then leaped to the ground and stalked beneath the tarp to the fire. Her wet fur stuck out in all directions. She began licking the mud from her coat. I stared at Allie. "What are you doing here?"

"Watching out for you. Since you wouldn't promise to watch out for yourself." Allie sullenly pulled off her pack, followed Tallow to the fire, and warmed her hands by the flames. Her face was smudged with dirt, her dripping hair loose and tangled. She pulled a chunk of bread from her pack and bit into it fiercely. "You two walk fast, you know that?"

Matthew looked at her, looked at me, then

silently filled a pot with water and put it on the fire. Allie huddled down near the flames. My stomach ached as I watched her. She seemed younger than I could ever remember being, too young to be out here. "I thought you weren't allowed Outside," I snapped, not knowing what else to say.

"Yeah, well, you're not allowed to go around slicing your hands open, either, and then tell me you can't even say it won't happen again." The firelight cast shadows on her face. "I'm your healer. You're my charge. I understand that, no matter what Dad or Caleb says. I can do what needs doing, too."

"You could have been killed out there. *Don't venture out alone into the dark...*"

"It wasn't dark when I left." Allie sank cross-legged to the ground and let Tallow into her lap. She petted the cat, smearing more mud on them both. "I didn't think you'd go without Tallow. That's why I hid her. But you left anyway, so we both had to follow. Tallow would never abandon *you*."

My hands shook. I couldn't find words. Beyond our shelter, rain fell steadily in the darkness. Matthew stared into the hissing pot, steam condensing on his nose and eyelashes. After a time, the water began to boil. He filled a metal mug, tossed in some tea leaves, and handed the mug to Allie. She clutched it tightly as Matthew poured cornmeal into the rest of the water.

"Your father will be worried," Matthew told her. "Did you consider that?"

Allie scowled into her tea. "Dad's always worried. He wants me to wait until I'm a little old lady to do anything."

"He wants you to be safe!" My voice rose. "You're going back at first light."

"I'll follow you again. As often as I have to. You're my charge."

"Did you leave word?" Matthew's voice was much calmer than mine. "Did you tell someone where you were going?"

"Of course not. I'm not stupid."

Matthew stirred the cornmeal with a metal spoon. "Listen, Allie. I left to follow Liza, too, so I understand about things that need doing.

135

But you have to let your dad know you're all right. I made sure my grandmother knew before I went."

Allie sipped her tea. "Did your grandmother try to stop you?"

"No. Gram was worried, she was frightened, but she understood."

"Your gramma's different, then. Dad would stop me. Caleb and Karin, too. All of them."

"They *should* stop you!" I said. "We're going as far from your safe town as anyone can go!"

Allie nodded fiercely. "I know. And I'm going with you. You need a healer anyway. It's dangerous out here."

"You don't know what danger is." I didn't have time for this. I needed to be thinking about Mom, not trying to keep this child safe. "We're taking you home."

Allie set down her tea and began working the tangles from Tallow's coat.

"Did you hear me?"

Allie scowled again as she looked up. "A healer can tell when a healing's not done. Things feel all unfinished, itchy beneath your skin, you know?"

"The only thing I know is that you're going home!" I grabbed her shoulders. She endangered us all — herself, me, Matthew, Mom — I realized I was shaking her only when she tried to twist free, and even then I couldn't seem to stop.

"Liza!" Matthew grabbed my shoulders and jerked me sharply away. Allie fell backward. She didn't cry out, just stared at me with wide, frightened eyes. Matthew whirled me to face him. "Liza, stop." His voice was lower now, like a growl. "You're not like this, Liza."

"Let me go," I hissed. Allie grabbed Tallow into her arms, but she didn't run away. Just like I'd always known better than to run away. I went limp in Matthew's arms. The damp firewood sizzled and popped. "I'm sorry," I whispered, but I couldn't meet Allie's eyes.

"You're not like him," Matthew said. He released me, and I drew my arms around myself.

"Go home," I told Allie. "Go back to your family. Go back where you're safe."

Allie lifted her chin, her face scared, defiant.

"You're not healed yet. I'm not going any-where."

* * *

I didn't speak to Allie for the rest of the night. I could barely bring myself to look at her. It was Matthew who made sure she ate, helped wash the mud from her skin and hair, and set her bedroll out by the fire.

When I offered to take the first watch, Matthew didn't argue. I stared at the sky, Tallow in my lap, watching the clouds scatter and the stars poke through. I kept a wary eye on the trees above the bluff, but if there were any tree shadows out tonight, I couldn't see them. Perhaps our fire kept them at bay.

A mockingbird called through the night, making a high hollow sound Father said echoed a car alarm. No matter that all the cars were rusted and silent—the birds remembered, and they passed the call on. Allie shivered, shedding her blanket. I scowled and drew it back over her. Her face scrunched up as if she worried at something in her sleep.

By now Samuel knew she was gone. Matthew

was right—he'd be worried. He'd be scared. I saw how he'd looked at her when she came through the Wall unharmed. He'd be searching for her.

What had Father done when I'd gone? Declared that I knew the rules and moved on? Or was he worried, too, even if he didn't let it show? I felt another surge of anger, forced it down, and paced until Matthew gently touched my shoulder and took over the watch.

*   *   *

I woke to Allie and Matthew talking. "You're still limping," Allie said.

"Not much."

"Want me to take a look?"

I opened my eyes to dawn light. My breath frosted in front of me as I sat up. Beyond the tarp the sky was clear, morning mist already thinning away. Allie knelt beside Matthew with her hands over his right leg and her face crinkled in concentration. "That's so strange. Like with Kimi—the injury isn't quite there. It's somewhere else, and without Caleb to show me where, I can't get at it."

"Don't worry about it." Matthew smiled and

shooed her hands away. "Given the shape I was in a couple days ago, I'll settle for a weak leg." He turned and drew a pot from the dying embers. The faerie folk could attack again tomorrow, and Matthew would continue boiling water, tending the fire.

He poured tea into plastic water bottles for later. Good plastic, not the kind that melted in the heat. I silently turned to packing our camp while Tallow threaded her way around my ankles and batted at bits of cooling ash caught by the breeze. "You're sure you won't let us take you back?" Matthew asked. Allie just shook her head. I said nothing. I still didn't trust myself to speak. I didn't want her to come, but in truth I had no idea how to stop her.

Allie had no trouble speaking as we shouldered our packs and started out into the cold, clear morning. "So big!" she said as she walked, all hints of the sullen child who'd found us gone. "Who knew the world was so big?" She twirled in place, right in the path, as if that world were the scene of a child's game, nothing more. Her hair had been braided back from her face, by her or by Matthew, I didn't know.

The sky dimmed as something crossed the sun. I froze, motioning Allie to stillness. Tallow hissed. Matthew made a low warning sound, like a whine at the back of his throat. Above the bluff a red-tailed hawk spread wings against the sky. A chill trickled down my spine. Once hawks had hunted only mice and rabbits, but no longer. Some said they'd bred with hawks from Faerie during the War. They were bigger now than they'd been, and they'd developed a taste for bigger game. Even as I watched, the hawk circled downward.

"Go away," I whispered fiercely, knowing I didn't have time to untie my bow. "Go *away*."

The hawk must have seen other prey. It veered abruptly back toward the bluff and disappeared amid the trees.

Allie fell silent for a time after that. The trees were quiet, too, as if their branches were as numb as the fingers I'd shoved into my pockets. A glow in the middle of the road caught my eye. "Look!" Allie said, seeing it at the same time. A stone the size of my fist, giving off faint purple light. "Just like Jared—"

"Don't!" I jerked Allie's arm back. *Don't touch any stone that glows.*

Allie pulled her arm away, seeming hurt. "I was only looking. I know better than to interfere with someone else's magic." She walked in a wide circle around the stone to prove the point. Matthew followed, wrinkling his nose as if he smelled something unpleasant. I went last. Even from the edge of the road I felt cold air brush my ankles. We passed a second stone, this one green, and a third, pale orange. "It feels cold the way healing feels cold," Allie said. The path narrowed and the stones grew more frequent. It was the lichens clinging to their surfaces that shone, I realized, not the rocks themselves. We veered uncomfortably close to the trees to pass them.

A white glow up ahead made us slow down. We turned a bend—and saw that a rockslide from the bluff blocked most of the trail. Dozens of the stones within it glowed white, as bright as sun on ice. Only a narrow corridor wound between the rocks and trees.

Matthew sniffed the air and started forward. Allie followed. I took up the rear, one hand on my knife. The oaks sighed faintly. The sun was rising, warming their green leaves.

A shadow darkened the rocks ahead. I looked up, even as the hawk screeched and dove for us. Allie froze, gaze turned upward, too startled to run. I threw myself over her, saw Matthew hit the dirt as well.

Around us, the stones exploded in a snow-bright blaze.

❧ Chapter 11 ❧

The hawk screeched again and fell silent. Pebbles rained down on my back. Somewhere, a wolf howled. A cat tongue licked my face.

I saw nothing but cold white light.

"Liza?" a voice whimpered below me. A hand reached for my own. I took it and squeezed hard. "Liza, I can't see."

"I'm here," I told Allie.

Teeth tugged at my sleeve, way too large for a cat. Tallow hissed and leaped to my back. The teeth let go. I heard an anxious whine.

"What's that?" Allie's voice was a child's voice, frightened at a bump in the dark.

I was frightened, too, but I didn't let her know that. "Matthew?" I whispered, reaching out my free hand.

The whining stopped and a damp nose shoved itself into my hand. No teeth this time, just skin and fur and the faint scent of fear. I moved my hand slowly up his nose, between his ears. His coat was rough at the surface, but softer beneath. I moved my hand to Matthew's back as I turned to stand by his side. Tallow hissed again and scrabbled up to my shoulders. With my other hand I urged Allie to her feet.

The wolf started forward but stopped when I didn't follow. "Can you see?" I asked him. No answer. No sound at all, save for soft panting. Tallow's claws dug through my sweater.

What choice did I have but to trust him and his magic? When he started forward again, I walked with him. Only Allie hesitated. "What about Matthew?" she asked, her hand still clutching mine.

"He's—here," I told her, realizing she didn't know. Even as I spoke I wondered how much of this wild creature really was Matthew and how much was something else.

Cold light pulsed against my eyes as we

walked. Allie's hand trembled in my own. Tallow's claws dug deeper. Only Matthew remained steady. I felt the rise and fall of his shoulders beneath my hand. Around us the trees whispered to one another. Farther off some animal wailed a childlike cry. Wind brushed my cheek.

"My eyes hurt," Allie said.

"Then close them." I kept my own eyes open, though. I saw a whisper of darkness against the light and strained to see better. In the distance I could just make out ash and cypress trees, their trunks tangled with ivy. Beyond the trees stood something darker and smoother. A metal arch, taller than any tree; it only seemed dark compared to the whiteness all around me. I quickened my pace, though according to Samuel's map we shouldn't be anywhere near the Arch.

The earth beneath the Arch trembled. A poison ivy vine swung overhead, and I ducked. I released my hold on Matthew's back and pulled Allie near. My knife was in my hand before I knew I'd drawn it.

Yet I felt no breeze as the vine passed by. I heard no sound. I felt no shaking beneath my feet, in spite of the trembling I'd seen. I looked slowly up.

The scene before me rippled like water. The trees faded, replaced by mounds of stone and twisted steel. The Arch rose above them, brighter now, smoke clinging like mist about its base. From somewhere beyond, a flock of metal birds flew toward the Arch, though the sound they made reminded me more of roaring water than of birds.

Airplanes, I thought. I knew then that what I saw wasn't real but only some reflection of the past; knew, too, that not all the airplanes had been brought down by magic after all. I shut my eyes but the vision remained.

Matthew woofed quietly, a question in the sound. I sheathed my knife and reached for his back while the airplanes flew at the Arch one by one, disappearing as their wings made contact with its bright surface.

"What's wrong?" Allie asked, and I knew neither she nor Matthew saw.

"Nothing," I whispered. "Nothing real." My heart pounded. The visions looked real enough. Matthew started forward again, and I followed, even as the scene shifted once more.

The Arch disappeared. I saw tall buildings, towers of glass and steel. From below, oaks stretched shadow branches toward the buildings. From above, hawks dropped stones that glowed with faerie light. Orange and white explosions lit the air. The buildings collapsed like a child's kindling towers.

My legs felt weak, as if they, too, might give way. I knew well enough I was seeing the War. I stumbled as a shower of glass tinkled to my feet, even as I told myself this wasn't real. I saw —

The road — a road of black stone — shuddering to life, shaking cars into ruins like a dog might shake off water.

Allie's grip on my hand tightened. Warmth flowed toward the faded knife scars on my palm. No, not warmth — gentler cold. I focused on that cold. I focused on the feel of Matthew's fur beneath my other hand. Slowly, the visions faded. I saw a gray outline beside me and realized it was a wolf, ears cocked forward, sniffing the air. I kept walking, and color bled through the brightness: green leaves, blue sky. All at once the white light was gone. I saw clearly the gray wolf beneath my hand. I looked back and saw Allie step through a wall of white light, not releasing my other hand as she did. The wall of light stretched to the sky, as tall as the buildings in my vision. The stones must have created it when they exploded. Had the faerie folk used stones and light like that to make our soldiers lose their way during the War?

Tallow's yellow tail lashed to and fro from my shoulders. Matthew's ears perked back. As I drew my fingers from his fur he turned to look at me, blinking. Matthew hadn't been able to see, either, I realized. He'd led us through by smell, not sight. I reached hesitantly toward him, but then Tallow hissed and I drew back. Matthew backed away, too, head lowered, ears flattening, a low growl rising in his throat. Allie glanced at him and silently moved to my side. The sun brightened. Silver light flowed over Matthew's gray fur. I waited for the boy to emerge from the wolf, for someone I could thank with human words. The light receded, but the wolf remained. He pawed the ground and whined.

"He's hurt!" Allie cried, even as I saw the blood on his hind leg. The gash had barely clotted, as if wild dogs had attacked us only moments before. Allie released my hand and darted forward.

"Wait!" I called, but she knelt and put hands to the wound.

The wolf whined again, with fear or with pain, but Allie's hands remained steady. "Oh!" she said. "Oh, but" — she shook her head — "healing first. Questions later."

Her tongue stuck out of the corner of her mouth as she focused on the wound. Light flowed from her hands over his leg. The wolf stretched his head around toward Allie, panting a little, his teeth so close — but he didn't hurt her.

I remembered how Matthew had scratched the air, threatening to kill, while Caleb had healed him. Beneath his easy smile, Matthew was as capable of anger as I was. He just controlled it better.

Allie's light faded. Old blood flaked away from an old wound. Allie leaned back on her heels, brown eyes thoughtful. "I didn't know you were a shifter, Matthew."

The wolf put weight on his leg, gingerly at first, then more steadily. He turned and nudged Allie's hands. She laughed. "You have a wet nose!"

He lifted his head, turning his gaze back to me. We regarded each other in silence. Finally I stepped forward, crouching in front of him. "Thank you," I whispered, wondering whether the words had any meaning to a wolf.

He nuzzled my chest with his nose. Tallow hissed and leaped from my shoulders. I ignored her and moved my hands to rest on Matthew's back. *So soft,* I thought. *How could wild magic feel so soft?*

"I only ever knew one shifter." Allie took Tallow in her arms, stroking the trembling cat. "But he was an owl. I think wolves are much nicer."

I looked into Matthew's eyes. Wild eyes, yet with an edge of fear behind them. "The other shifter you knew — what happened to him?"

"He flew away. Karin was his teacher. She said if only he'd come back, she'd have reminded him about being human. But I don't think Adam want-ed reminding. I think he liked to fly too much." The wall of light behind us made Allie's face seem very pale. We needed to move on, to put space between ourselves and that magic.

Yet I kept staring at Matthew. "Have you forgotten, too?" I asked.

Allie shook her head, hair falling from her braid into her face. "No. Matthew's still there. I could tell when I healed him."

"Then why can't he change back?"

"I don't know," Allie said. "Maybe it was that light. My hands are all itchy from it, like they're looking for something to heal. Maybe the light did something to Matthew's magic, too, made it stronger." She shook her head and shoved her hands into her pockets. "I don't know. This is closer to Karin's magic than mine or Caleb's. Things answer when Karin talks to them. We should bring him back to her " But Allie glanced at the glowing wall, then at me. We both knew we couldn't go back that way.

Something moved within the bright light. Some shadow — I blinked and it was gone. Perhaps it was only another vision. Perhaps not.

"We have to go on," I said, standing. Allie nodded. She reached for my hand and squeezed it, hard. Matthew sniffed at the trail as if he'd understood. "I'm sorry," I told him. Maybe he'd change back on his own. Or maybe Mom would know what to do. She knew about Matthew's magic, after all.

Knew and hadn't told me. I pushed the thought aside. Caleb's disk felt cold against my skin, another question. I ignored them both and started walking. Allie and Tallow followed me. Matthew followed them. We left the faerie light behind, save for a few glowing pebbles in the path. Even those disappeared after a time, but the cold lingered as the sun grew higher. My breath frosted in front of me again. Maybe that wasn't so strange, though. It was autumn, and in autumn the weather changed swiftly.

The path sloped uphill, leading us to the top of the bluff. Near sundown we came to a rusted car — there still were a few left along the roads — and camped there for the night. The seats were gone. The faint scent of car oil lingered in the chilly air, a scent from Before. Sometimes I tried to imagine a world where that smell was stronger than leaf mold and tree sap, but I always failed.

Allie and I spread blankets on the car's floor and strung our tarp over the empty windows. The glass was gone, of course, and the tires were cracked and dry. A short distance off, a fallen house lay half-buried beneath a gooseberry bush. I scavenged the exposed wood and built a fire near the car.

Allie fanned the flames as Tallow curled up in her lap. Matthew paced the borders of our camp. I watched him as I put water on the fire to boil. Every so often he'd stop and sniff the air. I wondered what he smelled.

I found some brown grasses by the old house and I twisted them between my fingers, making twine as I waited for the water to boil. The grasses were truly dead — they didn't moan as I worked them.

When the water bubbled I poured some cornmeal in, along with scraps of goat jerky. Matthew trotted to the fire, sniffed the pot curiously, and turned from it. I offered him a piece of jerky, but he nudged my hand away. His ears perked forward. He lifted his head, then whirled and bounded into the trees.

"Matthew!" Allie stood, dumping Tallow to the ground. I held up a hand, stopping her. In the distance, vines snapped and groaned. I heard a flurry of leaves, then silence. Allie looked at me, her eyes huge, but a few moments later Matthew trotted back to our fire, a rabbit dangling from his teeth. Blood stained the creature's white fur. Tallow took one look and bolted beneath the car.

Matthew dropped the rabbit at my feet, pride clear enough in the way he held his head and tail up high. As a human he'd never been much of a hunter.

Allie giggled nervously. "It's a gift."

I knew that, and I bowed my head to acknowledge it. "Thank you," I told the wolf. I took my knife and skinned the kill. Father had taught me how to skin game as soon as I was old enough to hold a knife, guiding my trembling hands with his steady ones, helping me to find the places between skin and muscle, sinew and bone.

I put some meat into the pot and offered Matthew the rest. He stalked a short way off to tear at the carcass. He wuffled happily as he ate, tail thumping the ground, saliva dripping from his teeth. By the firelight his eyes were bright. I thought of the boy Allie had known, the one who liked to fly. What if Matthew liked being a wolf more than being a boy? The snapping of bones between his teeth echoed the crackling and popping of the fire.

I took the pot from the flames and handed Allie a spoon. Much of our cookware was gone with Matthew's pack, so we shared from the pot instead. Allie's eyes kept darting to Matthew.

After dinner she spent a long time crouched by the old car, spoon in hand, urging Tallow to lick it clean, but the cat refused to come out. Matthew moved closer to the fire and slept, his breathing deep and satisfied.

"Which watch do I take?" Allie asked that night.

I started to say she was too young to take any watch, but she just looked at me, and I knew she was right. There was no one left to keep watch but us.

"I'll go first," I told her. From his place beside the fire Matthew watched us, head between his paws. Would he understand if we asked him to take a turn? There was no way to know.

Allie eyed me suspiciously. "You won't forget to wake me, will you? I'm still your healer, and I say you need sleep, too. I can help, no matter what Dad and Caleb say. You can trust me, you know."

"I know." I tousled her hair, like Mom had mine when I was little. I'd keep watch through the darkest part of the night, then wake her when the moon was high.

Allie finally coaxed Tallow out and took the cat inside the car with her. She handed a blanket out to me. I smiled a little, pulling the blanket around my shoulders as I climbed onto the car's hood to watch.

After a time Matthew climbed up beside me. He sighed, a sound as much human as wolf, and laid his head on my knee. I rested my hand behind his ears, and together we watched the moon rise, its light making the earth and car and trees all glow as if by magic.

*   *   *

By dawn frost coated the ground and made the dirt crunch beneath our feet. The trees were sleepy and slow, their branches barely moving in spite of the morning breeze. As we set out the path sloped downhill, leaving the bluff. Tallow rode on my shoulders, turning every so often to hiss at Matthew, who walked by Allie's side. Allie kept up a steady stream of chatter with the wolf, talking about her dad, about some fight she'd had with Kimi, about her training as a healer. "What I really wanted was to talk to animals," she confided. "I keep hoping. Karin says magic isn't always only one thing or another."

A bit later I heard her say, "Come on, Matthew, try it. One bark for yes, two barks for no." Matthew growled, as if barking on command was beneath his dignity. I couldn't help it—I laughed.

The sun rose, melting the frost. To the east, a glimmer of sun off water told us a river drew near. On Samuel's map, the river was called the Meramec. I went from shoving my hands into my pockets to tying my jacket around my waist in a matter of hours.

Midmorning the land opened out. Abruptly our path met a new road, broader than any I'd ever known, heading east. Thick slabs of black rock poked through the dirt, shimmering in the sun. According to Samuel's directions, this was I-44, and it would take us most of the way to the Arch. In the distance I heard running water.

We walked three abreast on that road, making a course for the river. Cinnamon-barked birches and pale gray cottonwoods lined our way. The birches launched clusters of tiny winged seeds into the breeze, but the road was so wide they drifted to the ground on either side of us. Birch seeds were too small to do any real harm, anyway, so long as you brushed them off before they could root in your skin.

We topped a rise and saw the Meramec River below. For a few hundred yards we descended toward the water, and then, all at once at the water's edge, the road ended. It continued on the river's other side, but a couple hundred yards of running water lay between us and the far bank. On our side, a few broken steel beams hinted at the bridge that had once spanned the distance. In the murky water around the beams, cattails splashed as they slapped at water striders. As far as I could tell the fuzzy brown stalks never hit the insects — it seemed more a game than anything else. A short way downstream, two tall metal poles stood across from each other, one on either bank. A pair of guide ropes was strung between them, one near the water, one several feet above. The ropes glinted in the sun, and when I drew closer I saw that they were metal as well, dozens of thin strands twisted into steel cord by someone from Before, more tightly than anyone could manage now. A mix of knotwork and metalwork bound the cords to the poles. I gripped the lower one — it felt strong and warm to the touch. It would hold our weight.

Matthew nosed at the shore. Allie looked from the ropes to the water and from the water to me. Her chatter fell silent, and her eyes went wide. "Maybe there's another bridge." Her voice was high and strange. "Check the map."

I shook my head. "The road ends here."

"Just check." The girl's voice cracked as she spoke.

I dug the map from my pack. The next crossing was at least a day's walk away, and there was no sign of a road to lead us from here to there.

"Too far," Allie said, but she looked up at me as if hoping for some other answer.

"There might not be a bridge there anymore, either," I said.

Allie nodded, looking unhappy. "What about Matthew? And Tallow?"

Tallow remained firmly seated on my shoulders, but Matthew poked a paw at the river. All at once he leaped in, swimming across in a splash of paws and wet fur. The current took him downstream a little. Once on land he trotted back upstream, put his nose to the ground, and looked at us across the water.

Watching him, Allie sighed. "Wish I was a wolf."

I looked at her, afraid to ask my next question. "You can swim, can't you?" Everyone could swim in Franklin Falls. Father and Kate had made sure of it.

Allie drew her arms around herself. "Don't know. Never tried."

She'd never been beyond the Wall. Of course she hadn't tried. I looked back the way we'd come. In the near distance, a small patch of road faded into shadow, sun no longer reflecting off its surface.

The sky was clear, no clouds blocking the sun. There shouldn't have been any shadows. Goose bumps prickled between my shoulders. As I watched the shadow crept forward, then drew back, as if uncertain.

It had followed me after all. If Allie hadn't been with me, I might have been glad I'd drawn it away from Washville. Instead I knew only that I had to get Allie across the river, where running water might protect her. "I'll go first," I said. "To test the ropes. But you have to follow as soon as I reach the other side, okay?"

Allie's braid had fallen over her shoulder.

She shoved it into her mouth and nodded again. I didn't waste any more time. I made sure Tallow was secure on my shoulders and my pack secure on my back, then grabbed hold of the upper rope and stepped onto the lower one.

The lower rope swayed a bit under my weight. I quickly shifted my balance and inched sideways across the river, moving first my right arm and leg, then my left. The upper rope dug into my palms, the lower into the soles of my boots, but the ropes were strong, sagging only a little beneath me. Halfway across water flowed over my boots, just for a few steps. Sooner than I had expected, I was on the other side. A wet wolf nose nudged my hands as I stepped onto land once more. Tallow hissed, leaped from my shoulders, and fled to the shelter of a dead log. I took off my pack, tugged my waterlogged boots from my feet, and turned back to Allie.

"Ready?" I called.

Allie didn't move. Her feet seemed firmly planted on the ground.

"It's all right," I said. "The ropes are fine."

Allie tugged at the straps of her pack and

chewed on the end of her braid. She stepped toward the ropes, then stopped, shaking her head. A cold wind picked up, blowing over the water. Instinctively I looked back to the road. Allie looked, too, and we both saw the shadow, only a stone's throw away from her now, flowing like a small dark puddle toward the river.

Matthew threw back his head and howled. The shadow halted, cowering like a frightened pup.

Allie scrambled onto the ropes. Her legs shook, making the lower rope sway. She had to stretch to reach the upper rope, which she clutched so hard her fingers turned white. She stood there, trembling, staring at me. Behind her the shadow moved forward again, but she didn't see.

I bit back the urge to yell, to scream, to tell her that we didn't have time. Instead I thought of Father, teaching me how to shoot an arrow. "Steady," I told Allie. "Steady and slow." I forced the doubts from my voice. "You can do this."

Allie inched out over the water, one slow, sliding step at a time. "Good," I told her. The wind picked up, making both ropes sway. "You're doing well."

The ropes sagged as she reached the middle. Her boots touched the water. She bit her lip and kept moving. I smiled, but she didn't smile back.

"That's it. Keep going. Just keep — "

Something green and slimy snaked out of the water, grabbing her ankle. Allie's hands lost their grip. She screamed and tumbled into the river, her pack falling from her back as she did.

I leaped in as Allie grabbed for the ropes and missed them. Her hair trailed in the water as she disappeared beneath the surface. Running water was supposed to stop magic, I thought wildly, plants and magic both. It was a rule, not one of Father's, but still a rule. Yet I knew better. Water hadn't stopped my visions, after all. Rules weren't promises, whatever we wanted to think.

I swam harder, fighting the current and diving beneath the water where Allie had fallen. I slashed at the green thing with my knife, slicing it in two. The upper half released its grip on Allie, but the lower half snaked out and wrapped itself around my wrist. My wrist went numb. I struggled to hang on to the knife.

I came up above the surface, sputtering for air. Treading water, I tore the thing free with my other hand. It came away with a soft squishing sound. It looked a little like a vine and a little like a wriggling green snake. I flung it from me and sheathed my knife as Allie floated to the surface a few feet away.

I swam to her, grabbed her around the chest, and kicked hard for shore. Allie coughed, too weakly to get up any water, and fell limp in my hold.

When we reached the bank, Matthew grabbed the back of Allie's shirt with his teeth and dragged her to shore. I stumbled after her, coughing and shaking.

Matthew nudged Allie with his nose. She didn't move. He whined, deep in his throat.

My heart pounded. I couldn't seem to get enough air. I rolled Allie over.

Her eyes were wide, unblinking. River water froze against my skin. I bent over her, pumping her chest, breathing air into her lungs the way Brianna the midwife had taught me. Allie didn't move. Her skin was clammy and far too cold.

"Come on, Allie." I pumped harder, the numbness in my wrist fading as I did. "Allie!" I called. My throat tightened around her name. *"Allie!"* My voice grew strange and deep, turning the words to a command. Light flashed at the edges of my sight. *"Allison!"*

She started coughing, heaving up water. I stopped pumping. Abruptly Allie sat up, hair dripping, blinking water out of her eyes. She threw her arms around my neck, shivering and gulping mouthfuls of air, clinging to me as if she would never let go. I held her until her shuddering slowed. She looked up at me then, not with fear, not with anger, but with wonder.

"You called me back," she said.

✌ Chapter 12 ✎

I built a fire for her in the middle of the road, scavenging what wood I could, repeating over and over, "I'm sorry, so sorry, I'm sorry ..."

Allie huddled by the flames with a blanket around her shoulders and Tallow curled in her lap. Matthew stretched out beside her. Wolf and cat both smelled of damp fur. For once they didn't seem to mind each other. "You *called* me," Allie said. There was awe in her voice. "I didn't know anyone could call so far."

I heard, didn't hear. "If Brianna hadn't taught me — how to pump the air back — I'm sorry — "

"It wasn't the pumping." Allie stroked Tallow's fur. I looked at them, looked away. "Listen, Liza." Allie's voice was low, not a child's voice. "You don't understand. I drowned there, and I died." I shook my head, but Allie went on, "No, I did. I'm a healer. I know when things are over, when there's nothing left to do. It's like falling through dark water and realizing you're too far down to ever get back out again. So dark — but I wasn't even angry, because I was too far down, though I was awfully sad. And then ..." Allie looked up at me. Matthew laid his paw on her ankle, as if for comfort. "Then you called me, Liza. And I had to listen. It was a long way out, but you kept calling, so I came. I was scared, I was tired, but I came."

The fire crackled and popped, but I felt as cold as Allie looked. I couldn't have called her back. No one could do that. Because if I could have called her, I also could have called — I also should have called ...

I felt colder still. I turned from Allie and the fire back to the river. The sun was high, the water bright. Across that water, at the end of the road, a dark shadow lay puddled in the light. It flowed toward me, then stopped, as if an invisible wall rose out of the river. A sound started up: a low, frightened cry.

A baby's cry.

Matthew moved to my side. His ears went back. He regarded the shadow across the water and squeaked softly, as if asking some question. The shadow just kept crying.

"Who is she?" Allie whispered. "Did you — did you call her, too?"

"I didn't call anyone." But the shadow kept crying, the sort of short choking sobs babies make when they know something's wrong but they can't tell you what. I wanted to run, to hide — but I knew I couldn't escape that sound any more than I could escape the memory of bones on a moonlit hillside.

I felt Allie's hand on my shoulder and flinched as if burned. "You can't leave her there," Allie said.

"Go away," I told her.

"She's just a baby, she doesn't understand — "

"Go *away!*"

Allie scuttled backward as I turned, her eyes wide, and I realized I'd put command into the word, the same command I'd used to call her back. I felt as if something dark were coiled inside me behind that command. A wrong word, a wrong gesture, and I would set it loose, free to destroy as the faerie folk had destroyed. I clenched my hands into fists, forcing the tension inward. Allie sighed and stopped backing away.

She was the one who didn't understand. My sister was dead. I'd seen Father take her away. I'd seen the cracked, bloody bones that were her only remains. Even those bones were likely gone now, eaten or buried by some wild creature. No one could call anyone back after that. No one had that kind of power, not the faerie folk, not humans — no one.

Yet the shadow cried on. My fingernails dug into my palms, drawing blood. The pain released the coiled tension, giving it somewhere to go. I thought of the knife at my belt. For just a moment, I wished Father were here— to take that blade, to put an end to me and my magic, to keep me from having to face the shadow that waited on the other side of the river. I moved my hand to the hilt, taking comfort in its familiar grip.

A wet nose nudged my hand away. I looked up, into gray wolf eyes. I reached out, meaning to shove Matthew away.

Instead I found myself grabbing him, holding him. I fell to my knees, clutching his fur like Allie had clutched the ropes, not daring to let go. "It's not my fault," I whispered. Then, louder, "It's not my fault!" My screams drowned out the choking baby cries behind me. "There was nothing I could do once Father decided! You know that, you were there!" My fingers dug into his fur, surely causing pain, but the wolf remained silent, steady.

"Matthew." I spoke his name aloud, thinking of the gray wolf, the quiet boy, knowing that they were the same. "You were there, Matthew." I shivered as I spoke, feeling the power beneath the words, understanding them for the call they were.

Fur shrank from my grasp. My fingers dug into Matthew's bare shoulders as he knelt before me. Still he didn't draw away. Human arms reached out and held me. My trembling subsided. "It isn't your fault," Matthew repeated gently. "It's his fault, Liza, not yours."

I remembered running from the hillside where Rebecca had died, screaming her name as I did. I'd called her as surely as I'd called Allie. "But I was too late." My voice was flat and cold, the truth of the fact seeping into my bones. I could have called Rebecca back, if only I'd gone sooner. I even could have carried her back without magic, if only I'd arrived in time.

Matthew looked at me, but there was no blame in his human eyes. Sunlight shone on his skin and loose hair. I drew back and stood, feeling a faint flush through everything else as I thought of how I'd held him, unashamed. Allie got the raincloak from my pack and draped it over his shoulders. He pulled it absently around himself as he stood. "You didn't know," he said.

But I knew now. Knew that I'd been too late but had called Rebecca back anyway. Knew that she'd answered that call, as much as she was able. Knew that I was responsible for the shadow that had followed me from home, touched Kimi, and forced Allie across the river.

I walked to the river's edge and knelt to gaze at the patch of darkness on the other side. The cries gave way to gasping, troubled breaths.

"Rebecca," I whispered, and she fell silent at

my voice.

Allie was right. I couldn't leave her there. "Rebecca," I called, louder, putting command into the word. *"Rebecca!"* My throat tightened around that call.

The shadow surged forward, drew back. Then it shuddered, rose up, and flew across the water, gliding toward me like a small dark bird. I opened my arms. The shadow flew into them, and I drew it close. Shadow overflowed my arms like an old blanket.

It was only a shadow. It had no weight, but it felt cold as ice. The cold didn't chill me, though, not like it had Kimi. This was my magic, I realized. I could handle it, as surely as Jared could handle his glowing stones.

Jared's stones had burned him. I remembered Karin saying that.

Still I carried the shadow to the fire. As I knelt by the flames it took shape, bits of gray resolving into misty legs that kicked at the air and misty fingers that flailed for something to grasp. Downy hair covered the shadow's head, not faerie pale now but cast in shades of gray. Dark eyes blinked up at me. The baby scrunched her face and began to cry again, even as her weight settled into my arms. Somehow I knew that no one else would feel that weight—their hands would pass right through her. This was my magic. It was my responsibility.

I rocked Rebecca in my arms. I could see right through her scrunched-up face to where my hand cradled her head. A warm breeze blew. I wrapped Rebecca in my jacket and shifted her to my shoulder. She was larger than I remembered, but not by much.

"I can't heal this," Allie said. "Caleb told me some things I couldn't heal, but I didn't understand. What do we do with her, Liza?"

"We'll take her to Mom," I said, having no other answer.

Matthew nodded. Tallow sniffed his fingers suspiciously. If any wolf scent remained, though, she forgot it as soon as Matthew scratched her behind the ears. His hand moved slowly, and he stared at his fingers, as if getting used to being human again.

I gave him my spare clothes. The sweater

strained across his shoulders, and the pants ended well above his ankles. His feet remained bare, because I didn't have extra boots.

Allie and I walked barefoot, too, our boots and socks tied to the pack to dry in the sun. I gave Allie the raincloak, which trailed behind her. Our clothes remained damp in spite of the fire, but we had no others left to wear. At least the sun was high. Our clothes would dry as we walked.

Silently I scattered the fire and threw dirt on the coals. Matthew tied the pack closed and swung it onto his back. Allie put Tallow on her shoulders. I took Rebecca, the one thing no one else could carry. We walked swiftly away, agreeing without words to put as much distance between ourselves and the river as we could.

After a time Rebecca's sobs subsided and she seemed to sleep, with her cold cheek pressed against my shoulder. If not for that cold, I could almost have forgotten she wasn't alive. I ran a finger along the back of her head. Her soft shadow hair was cool as wool beneath frost.

We walked through the rest of the day and

into dusk. When the sky grew too dim we camped in the road, away from the trees to either side. I piled dirt under my jacket before I laid Rebecca down. Her feet kicked the air as she slept on. Tallow batted at her ankles, drew back as if at cold water, and stalked off to follow Matthew as he scavenged wood from the road-side.

"Your hands." Allie said sharply.

I looked down. The green river creature had left no mark, but my palms were torn and red where I'd dug my fingernails in. Allie took my hands in her own, running her fingers over the gashes. Silver light shimmered on my palms, then sank beneath the skin, taking the redness with it and leaving a faint chill behind.

"With all you can do," the girl said, "you could at least take care of yourself."

Rebecca slept through dinner that night, and through Matthew's watch as well. The moon was high and my own watch nearly through when she woke and started crying again. I took her in my arms and rocked her, ignoring the cold I felt. I sang songs Mom had sung to me when I was small.

"Sleep my child, and peace attend thee,
All through the night …"

Allie stirred, cast her blankets aside, and padded over to us. "She cries so much," the girl said.

My singing trailed to silence. I couldn't remember all the words. Rebecca fidgeted in my arms. "That's what babies do."

Allie knelt and tossed pieces of dead grass into the fire. I'd been planning to make rope from them. "She's crying because she doesn't want to be dead."

Rebecca gripped my thumb and fell silent. Her hold was surprisingly strong. I saw my own finger through her fist.

"I'm a healer," Allie said stiffly. Her eyes were on the flames, not me. "I've seen people die. Caleb says you have to know when to let go and when not to. He says it's harder than knowing when to break a fever or set a bone.

The patient doesn't always know the right time, but neither does the healer. I don't know how Caleb decides. I don't know how I'll decide when I have to."

I rocked Rebecca until she stopped fidgeting and her breath deepened into sleep. I wished I had an extra blanket. I wished a blanket or jacket were enough to keep her warm. "Your watch?" I asked Allie. She'd insisted on taking one again.

Allie looked to the sky. Scraps of cloud drifted over the moon. "I'm glad you called me back, Liza. But next time you might want to ask first. Because for someone else it might be different. And the healer can't decide alone."

* * *

Our food was low with the loss of Matthew's and Allie's packs, so at dawn I went hunting. Samuel's bow served me well. I loosed my arrow with hardly a sound, bringing down a chubby woodchuck that would feed us for a couple days. When I returned to camp, Matthew and Allie were setting up a spit to cook the meat, as if they hadn't doubted my success.

Matthew grinned. "Figures you'd beat my

rabbit. You always were the better hunter." I remembered that rabbit dangling from Matthew's jaws, remembered the sound of his teeth tearing fur and crunching bone. If the thought made Matthew uneasy he gave no sign, just asked for my knife so he could skin the woodchuck. I left him and Allie to that job and checked on Rebecca. She slept wrapped in my jacket, her arms and legs curled inward as if for comfort. At my approach she smiled but kept sleeping.

I fashioned my raincloak into a sling so that I could carry her with me as I worked. She was only shadow, I told myself—but I'd felt strange leaving her behind when I hunted.

We spent the morning cooking the meat and then carving it. We stored it in the same plastic containers where Samuel had packed the jerky and cornmeal, yellowed containers that cracked if you handled them wrong but whose lids sealed well otherwise. The meat would only keep a day or two, but we'd likely finish by then, anyway.

We left a little after noon. Matthew took the pack again, Allie took Tallow, and I carried

Rebecca. If Samuel's map was right, the Arch was less than two days away.

Glowing stones appeared in the road again, lit shades of orange and red, green and blue. Sometimes the road's black rock glowed as well. We slowed down, keeping watch for those lights as we walked. Rebecca slept, cried, slept again. A few stray strands of my hair fell into her face, and when I drew them away they were clear instead of black.

The road narrowed. Maples and sycamores stretched branches overhead, sun turning the edges of their leaves to gold. Had autumn been like this Before, green leaves turned to fire as if by the light? Bright maple seeds twirled to the ground, trailing sparks behind them. Saplings grew through cracks in the black stone, slowing us further as we walked around them, staying out of reach of their young branches.

The sparks faded as the afternoon progressed. We reached a wider stretch of river. The bridge was gone here, too, but rockfalls had dammed the water. The crossing was difficult, but we managed. Allie clung to my hand all the way.

On the river's far side we began a long, slow climb. Near the crest of a hill another road crossed ours. On the map there were more roads here, and they looped around each other in a complicated cloverleaf pattern, but there was no sign of that cloverleaf now. Light reflected off the dust in the air, making the place shimmer. The light brightened, and I looked away. I didn't want more visions.

Yet as we reached the middle of the crossroads, light exploded behind my eyes. I fell to my knees, rubbing my temples, willing pain and light to go away. Rebecca wailed, but the sound faded as the light brightened. In that brightness I saw —

Black roads buckling like leather, tossing away the cars that rode their surface. Roots breaking through black stone, twisting metal until blood streaked the steel like a child's mud paintings —

People running alongside tall buildings, falling as roots broke through the earth at their feet. Dirt churning like flour in a sieve, and the people slipping from view one by one, their hands grasping air to the last, leaving behind only dirt and roots and jagged bone —

Men and women with pale hair and silver eyes, chanting commands that brought light to stone, that made trees bend and sway, giving them strength, making them reach high and dig deep —

Screaming, screaming everywhere, choked to silence, choked to dust —

I screamed as well. Someone shook me. I pushed through the visions like a swimmer through water. Allie looked anxiously down, her hands on my shoulders. Tallow trembled against her neck. In the sling, Rebecca cried on.

I looked to the earth at my knees, knowing now what lay beneath it. Blood and bone, metal and glass, all tangled with deep roots. The trees around this clearing had fed well during the War. When I looked up, I saw ropey shadows stretching from their branches toward us, not quite long enough to reach.

I heard a strangled sound and saw Matthew bent over beside me, retching. I stumbled to my feet, reached into the pack he carried, and handed him a water bottle. He drank, coughed the water up, and drank again.

"I can smell them," he rasped. His face was

very pale. "God, Liza, you can't believe the smell."

"And I can feel them," said Allie as she took Tallow in her arms and rocked back and forth. "So many people. This will never be right. This will never be healed."

Something cold tugged my boot. I looked down and saw a shadow hand reaching out of the hill. I jerked away, but the shadow followed, stretching like rubber from Before. My stomach churned. I walked away, and after several steps the hand lost its grip and snapped back to earth. But still I felt it calling me. No, not calling. Yearning to be called. The shadows beneath this hill didn't want to be dead.

I walked faster. Matthew and Allie followed right behind. Tears streamed down Allie's cheeks while Matthew looked as if he might be ill again any moment. Rebecca kept crying. I rocked her as I walked, not sure which of us I sought to comfort.

Wind blew around my ankles as we descended the hill. I didn't look down. I knew I'd see more human shadows aching for my call. Something in me ached with them. I held Rebecca close, not caring about the cold that seeped through my sweater.

The shadows beneath my feet subsided as we left the crossroads behind and continued along our road, which veered northeast. Rebecca sighed and fell silent. But the ropey tree shadows around us grew, lengthening as shadows do near sunset and hissing as they swung through the air. We walked on, not willing to camp amid those shadows and not willing to return to the crossroads. Light faded around us. The sun touched the horizon, and the clouds turned gold above the treetops.

"How much they must have hated us," Matthew said.

"Who?" Allie asked. I heard Tallow purring on her shoulders.

"The faerie folk. To have done this."

"But the fey ..." Allie hesitated.

I looked to the orange horizon. I looked to the swaying trees and their shadows. Had those trees really been safe Before? "The faerie folk weren't human. Of course they hated us." Us and all we'd built.

"But they didn't ..." Allie sounded puzzled. "I mean — they were no worse than we were Liza!"

"What?" How could anyone, seeing the world as it was now, say that? Did Washville teach its children nothing? "You know all that the faerie folk did to us." I remembered the men and women in my vision, chanting power to the trees. Men and women with clear hair and silver eyes. Men and women like — I stopped abruptly and turned. "Caleb," I said. "Karin, too." Caleb who walked so quietly I never heard him coming. Karin who saw clearly even in the dark.

"Of course," Allie said. "I thought you knew. Dad thought so, too. How else could they know so much about magic?"

I'd assumed they were just humans touched by magic, like Matthew and Allie and me. The faerie folk were supposed to be monsters, with dark wings and gnarled tree-bark hair. They weren't supposed to look just like us.

"But Karin fought in the War," I said, feeling stupid.

"Yes," Allie agreed. "But, Liza, she didn't fight for us."

I tried to picture Karin chanting to the trees, bringing the buildings down, watching as my people died. My throat hurt. "Karin saved our lives." *Trees have always listened to me, since I was a child.* How long ago had that been? In the old stories the faerie folk lived forever.

Matthew reached out to scratch Tallow behind the ears, his expression troubled. It wasn't just me—he hadn't known, either. Matthew turned to the side of the road, pulling a dead branch from a hawthorn thicket but backing away before the living branches could slash at him. He took a sharp stone and began scraping bright orange mushrooms off the stick. The mushrooms glowed faint green, not poisonous but enough to make one ill. "We need torches if we're to walk much farther," he said.

Tallow jumped from Allie's shoulders and batted at the falling mushrooms. "The fey folk lost as much as we did during the War," Allie said. "You both know that, don't you? Everyone knows that."

I wasn't sure what I knew. I took the pack from Matthew and rummaged through it, finding the plastic torch Samuel had given me. I showed Matthew how to use it, then doused the light. Samuel said the batteries would lose strength over time, and we had only one spare set. Matthew took the torch and set his stick aside. We walked on in silence while the horizon faded to pink. Rebecca's breath felt cold against my neck.

Allie said, "Everyone was a little crazy during the War. That's what Dad says."

Tree shadows narrowed the path. We walked single file between them. "My father says the War only showed people for what they really were," I told her.

"He would know," Matthew said, but when I glanced sharply back he looked away.

I stepped around a stone that glowed dandelion yellow. "Father saved our town." Father and Kate had held Franklin Falls together during the War, and during the looting that followed, too. They'd brought back the old skills, like bow hunting and weaving and farming without machines. When outsiders threatened us, Father organized the townsfolk to turn them away. When magic was born among us—

I glanced down at Rebecca. "Father had no choice." Yet Rebecca hadn't done any harm with her magic, any more than Allie or Jared had.

"The War is over," Matthew said. "Ian doesn't understand that."

"Over?" I felt something cold through my boots and looked down as a stray shadow hand released its grip and sank into the earth. How could anyone say this was over? "If it was over Cam couldn't have ..." My words trailed to silence even as Matthew stopped and looked right at me. I stopped, too. There was nothing casual in the hunch of Matthew's shoulders now.

"Who's Cam?" Allie's voice squeaked as she looked uneasily back and forth between us.

"Cam was my brother," Matthew said. He kept staring at me, his gaze so dark that I knew I didn't want to see what would happen if his anger ever did slip beyond his control.

"Oh," Allie breathed softly. Then, just as soft, "You don't have any teachers in your town, do you?"

"No," I told her.

"Yes," Matthew said. I glanced back again—
what teachers?—but this time he ignored me. "Not
the sort of teachers you have, though," he told
Allie.

Allie nodded soberly, as if that explained a
lot. I started walking again, faster than before. A
moth fluttered past me, bright wings vibrating.
Rebecca lifted her head and reached for it, but
her hand passed right through. The moth
flickered out. Rebecca smiled as if she were an
ordinary baby. My throat felt suddenly dry.

The road narrowed further. I stopped
abruptly.

Ahead of us tree shadows crossed the road,
weaving themselves into a net and filling the
way with darkness.

❧ Chapter 13 ❧

I turned around. The way behind was dark, too. The only light seemed to be the twilight around us, which was already fading to gray. Matthew fumbled with the plastic torch. It flared to life, producing a wide beam of light. That should have dispelled the shadows nearest us, but they drew closer to the light, as if for warmth.

"Ow!" A length of shadow lashed at Allie's arm. She jerked back. Blood soaked through a jagged gash in her sleeve. She pressed her hand against it, muttering words I hadn't thought she knew.

Another shadow snaked around the torch. The torch sizzled like wet firewood, flickered, and went out. Around us, trees began to groan. Something cold slashed my cheek, breaking skin.

"*Go away!*" I shouted.

The shadows drew back. The trees fell silent. The twilight brightened around us.

Matthew drew a breath. "Keep saying it, Liza. Just— keep saying it."

I did so, chanting like a child afraid of the dark. "*Go away.*" Matthew lit the torch once more. "*Go away, go away, go away.*" The shadows kept their distance, staying a few dozen yards back on all sides.

Magic flows in both directions, Karin said. If I could call things to me, I could also push them back.

"*Go away.*" We walked on. I kept ordering the darkness back, and it kept retreating. That darkness happily would have swallowed us whole, if not for my words.

If not for my magic.

"*Go away.*" Rebecca shifted in her sling and reached for my hair. Allie walked as close behind me as she could, her footsteps landing where mine had been. Her braid was in her mouth again, and she chewed it as she walked. On her shoulders, Tallow hissed and swiped at something in the dark. Behind them, Matthew's movements were slower, more fluid, even as he hunched beneath the pack.

"Go away." I prayed Matthew was right that magic could be controlled. Because my magic was all that stood between us and the dark.

*   *   *

We walked through the night. My voice grew hoarse as time passed. For a while the white torchlight held, much steadier than oil or burning wood.

Bluffs rose to either side of us, holding shadows of their own: a shadow arm with a dangling charm bracelet, a shadow boot kicking the air as if to get free, a shadow face staring at us from within a hillside, its mouth open as in surprise, a poplar root growing through one of its shadow eyes.

When the torchlight dimmed from white to yellow and then went out, we quickly changed the batteries in the dark while I shouted as loudly as I could to keep the trees away. My throat ached after that, and my chest, too, but I didn't stop.

"*Go away.*" I thought of Mom, alone in this darkness with no magic to protect her. Yet if my visions were true, somehow she'd found a way through to the Arch.

An owl hooted, but it, too, kept its distance. The moon rose, casting thin beams of light through the dark web around us. Rain began to fall, soaking my hair and turning the road to mud. That rain fell right through Rebecca and puddled beneath her in the sling. I drew the raincloak over her.

The trees started moaning again, stretching toward the water but drawing back at my words. The air grew chill, from rain or shadows, I couldn't tell. Clouds covered the moon.

"*Go away.*" Each word took strength. As if it weren't only my words but something deeper inside me that pushed the shadows back. I grew weary with the effort of that pushing.

Ahead, through gaps among the shadows, I saw patches of pale light.

Dawn. My legs went weak at the sight. I stumbled but kept speaking. Allie bumped into me and let out a startled cry. Rebecca started awake and made small fussy sounds.

I rocked her as I kept walking. My legs felt heavy as stone, but I didn't dare stop. The road turned north. Water carved rivulets through the mud and around patches of black rock. Each step, each word, took more work than the last. I struggled to keep my eyes open and my lips moving. "*Go away.*"

The rain let up. The clouds pulled apart like carded wool. Sunlight set the clouds ablaze just as our torch dimmed to yellow again. Matthew clicked it off. To the east, beyond the bluffs, light glinted off distant water.

Something else shone in the distance ahead. A silver rainbow, beginning amid the trees but arching high above them. Silver drew my gaze up and up, even as I caught my breath. Metal reflected the morning sun, far brighter than Kate's mirror. I forced my gaze away, though I yearned to keep looking upward.

"So that's the Arch," Allie whispered.

Just like in my visions. Just like on Caleb's disk. "Mom," I said, and tried to walk faster.

My legs wouldn't listen. It was all I could do

to keep lifting first one, then the other. Rebecca's sling dug into my shoulder. The road climbed toward the top of the bluffs. Up ahead, another road met it.

This crossroads formed a larger clearing than the last. Slabs of black stone shone in the sun. I staggered as I neared its center, but no shadows of the dead reached for me from under this hill. No visions filled my sight. Ash and cypress stretched shadow branches toward us, but the clearing was too wide. The shadows couldn't reach.

I fell to my knees and let my voice go silent. Maybe I could afford to rest here, just for a moment.

Matthew knelt beside me. I leaned, trembling, into his arms, barely remembering to shield him from Rebecca with my own arms as I did. I was so very tired.

"Liza." Matthew's arms tightened around me. He smelled of rain and wet wool. "You got us through."

I shook my head. "Not yet." There was still more forest and more shadow between us and the Arch. We had to keep walking. I stumbled to my feet, took a few steps, and fell again. Allie cried out. This time she and Matthew both helped me lie down.

I tried to sit up and felt Matthew's firm hand on my shoulder. "If anyone could go on it'd be you, Liza. But even you need to rest after a night like that."

I shook my head, but when I closed my eyes, I couldn't find the energy to open them again.

"Don't worry," Matthew said. "I'll keep watch."

I didn't have the strength to protest any further. Yet even in sleep I felt the trail beneath my feet and saw shadows reaching for me out of the dark.

*   *   *

I woke what seemed moments later and found the sun past noon. I shifted Rebecca's weight gently as I sat up. Her cold hand brushed my cheek.

Matthew handed me a water bottle. I drank deeply. My throat hurt when I swallowed. "Thank you." My voice came out scratchy and dry.

"Thank you," Matthew said. "For keeping us

alive last night."

Allie slept on a blanket beside us, her face resting on one hand. Tallow was pressed up against the girl's back with a paw tangled in her hair, which had mostly fallen out of its braid.

The tree shadows were gone now that the sun was up, and any human shadows remained beneath the earth, beyond calling or wanting to be called. This crossroads was nowhere near as bad as the other one, whether because fewer people had died here or because they'd died more completely, I didn't know.

I stood, stretching my legs—and caught my breath.

From the hilltop I clearly saw both River and Arch.

The River lay downslope to the east, so close I almost could have shot an arrow to it. The Mississippi—it made the Meramec look like little more than a creek. By the near shore willows trailed branches into the water. The far shore was a half mile away, maybe more. Between the banks green-brown water flowed relentlessly south, ribbons of light rippling on its surface. I stared, but no visions caught me. No magic of mine could stop this River's flow to make it reflect like metal or glass. I heard the River's murmur even from where I stood. My breathing slowed to match the sound.

The Arch lay upstream, a quarter mile north at most, towering above the trees that surrounded it. Bright as a mirror, tall as a dozen trees — sun glinted off its highest point, and I looked swiftly away. The Arch could catch me in visions without half trying, and once it caught me I wasn't sure it would let go. It had to be magic. No one could build or grow anything like that.

"Impressive, isn't it?" Matthew handed me some woodchuck and I chewed hungrily, my gaze returning to the River as I did.

Allie yawned, stood, and walked to my side. She reached for my hand. "We don't have to cross that one, do we?" Her voice sounded very small.

I shook my head. No one could cross that River, and no bridge could span it, not without the River's consent. But we didn't need to cross it. We only needed to reach the Arch. I drew Caleb's disk out and thoughtfully traced the Arch inscribed there.

"Why'd Caleb give you that, anyway?" Allie asked. "I never even knew he had it before."

"I don't know." That was one of my questions for Mom when I found her. Not my first question, though. My first question was why she'd left me in the first place.

"Come on," I said. "We should go while the sun's high."

Matthew, Allie, and Tallow followed me across the clearing and down the other side of the hill. Huge bluffs rose to the west once more, but to the east the forested land was level. Beyond the trees, the River murmured on. I found my steps drifting toward it, forced myself away, and found myself drifting again. Rebecca fidgeted uneasily.

Allie stepped right off the road, and Matthew pulled her back. Allie fought him a moment, then shook her head like a sleepwalker waking. "The River's calling me," she said. "Just like Liza called me. It says I had no right to escape the way I did.

It says I have to go back."

Matthew growled softly and tightened his grip on her arm. I turned toward the water. "*Go away*," I said as firmly as I could.

More firmly the River murmured back, *Come here.*

Sweat trickled down my face, though the air was cool. I stepped toward the water without realizing it and drew back with effort. Rebecca started to cry, and her cries were timed to the River's flow.

Come, Liza. Let us finish what we started. In one of my daughter rivers, not so long ago, you sought my darkness.

I pushed my heels down firmly against the road. If I could keep shadows back through the long night, I could resist the River's call.

"I don't hear it," Matthew said. But then he'd never come close to drowning, not like Allie and me.

"Watch Allie," I told him, and I started walking again. Not toward the water. Along the road toward the Arch.

Come, Liza. Seek silence, seek darkness, seek rest.

I lifted one foot at a time, the way Father had taught me for hunting, pressing it firmly back to the ground ahead before lifting the other.

After only a couple hundred paces the road ended, leaving only forest between us and the Arch. I slowly came to a stop, ignoring Rebecca's cries as she grabbed at a lock of my hair. The Arch was very close now, and very bright. I craned my neck to glance at the top of it. Its legs were hidden by trees, but they must have been hundreds of feet apart, as far apart as the Arch was tall.

Beside me Matthew kept hold of Allie's hand. Tallow twined around their feet. Allie's lips were pressed tightly together, her eyes closed, as if she fought something I couldn't see. I could feel it, though, tugging at some place deep inside me. Ebb and flow, ebb and flow, one small tug after another. *Come, Liza.*

"We have to go through the forest," I said. Matthew nodded.

Slowly I led the way among the trees, pressing each foot deep into the dirt as I set it down. Ash and cypress didn't seem concerned with us, though. The trees bent toward the River, moaning softly, stretching their branches downward. I yearned to turn toward the water as well, but I kept walking forward instead.

Behind me Allie screamed. Tallow bolted past. Even then I moved slowly, digging my boots into the soil before I turned my head. Matthew held Allie beneath the armpits. The girl bit and kicked, trying to get away. "It's calling!" she cried. "You don't understand. It's calling and I have to listen. I have to!"

Matthew struggled a moment to balance girl and pack. "It's all right. I won't let her go."

I nodded and forced my attention back to my own steps. One more step. Then another. And another. I lifted my left foot out of the dirt and onto bleached stone. My right foot followed a moment later. Water lapped at more stone just a dozen yards away. A few more steps and I stood beside the base of the Arch. I kept going, walking around to its inner edge.

The air about me shimmered with sound, a low hum that muffled the River's call. Rebecca fell silent and pressed her fists against my chest.

Metal shone beside me, above me—even the base of the Arch was many times wider than I was tall. The humming grew louder, echoing uncomfortably between my ears. I kept my gaze carefully to the ground, though I ached to look up. Sun and metal made me dizzy.

Allie fell silent as Matthew came up beside me. Her hands clutched his sweater, as if now she was the one who didn't want to let go. Tallow followed them, sniffing the stone suspiciously.

Come. The River's pull was weaker beneath the Arch and easier to resist. The Arch's metal surface stood only an arm's length away.

Would I find Mom on the other side of that metal? Would I find a way through at all?

I looked at Matthew. He set Allie down, and she clutched his hand even as he grabbed for her. Tallow scrambled up onto Allie's shoulders. Together Matthew, Allie, and I stepped forward, praying the way would be open and the Arch would let us through.

The metal remained metal, nothing more. I pressed it, I pounded it, but it didn't give. I drew a deep breath. Karin had said I might have to rely on my visions, but Mom had found a way through without visions, hadn't she? She'd held that veined metal disk in her hand and spoken some words.

Mom had that disk all her life. It couldn't be magic.

I took Caleb's disk in my hand and reached out again. The metal still didn't give. If there were words I needed to speak, I didn't know them. The Arch grew bright at my gaze, as bright as a mirror and brighter still. "Lizzy," Mom whispered. I reached for her, then drew sharply back.

And reached out again. The metal was as solid as it ever was. But a moment before—when Mom had called me—my hand had passed right through, just like Karin had said it would.

"How—" Allie said. "How did you—"

Karin had also said that if I failed, I could wander in visions forever. I glanced at Matthew and Allie. I might not be the only one trapped if something went wrong.

Matthew shrugged. "Your magic got us this far."

I swallowed hard. "Even if I make it through,

you might not be able to follow me. And even if you follow me—"

"I trust you," Matthew said.

"You don't understand." My fear turned to anger. "I have no idea what will happen. Even if we don't get lost in my visions, we could get stuck in the metal, or give in to the River, or wind up someplace else, who knows where—my magic could kill us all!"

"He didn't say he trusts you to know everything." Allie twisted Matthew's sweater sleeve around her wrist, stretching it. "No one knows that. You just do what you can, you know? And see what happens after that."

I drew Rebecca close, shivering. The baby squirmed in my hold. I hadn't done all I could for her. Or else I'd done it too late. I might be too late for Mom, too.

Rebecca reached out and tugged at my hair. I looked down at her. She smiled, and I swallowed hard. Until I knew I was too late, I had to do what I could.

Matthew took my hand. His grip was steady and comforting—I focused on it as I looked into the metal, willing the visions to come. For a moment I saw only my own reflection — dark hair streaked with paler strands — and then —

Light. Light bright as moonlight, light that pulsed against my eyes. I fought not to press knuckles up against my lids. "Mom," I called, and then, louder, "Mom!"

Fire. Fire rained from airplanes and fell toward swaying branches. Heat burned my face, like the air from Jayce's forge. Leaves gave way to flame as if they were no more than butterfly wings. Branches blazed like torches and went out. Acorns fell like rain. Berry juice stained the dirt and evaporated in the hot, dry wind. Trees moaned as they died, like wind before a storm —

Fire mushroomed up from the earth, swallowing men and women with clear hair and silver eyes, so fast they made no sound. Ash fell to the ground for miles around, silent as snow. No bone or branch remained —

Farther from the fire, a few black trunks survived, jutting like splinters from the earth. Caleb — why always Caleb? — walked through the dead land, his face grim. He approached a burning lake, stepped into the water, and disappeared —

My mother walked through the dead land, her cheeks streaked with ash, her head bowed like a tree in the wind. Even as I reached for her she fell to her knees. Her face shone orange, lit by flames. I shut my eyes, retreating into darkness. Wind burned the back of my neck —

"Liza," Matthew said, still holding my hand. His voice sounded dry and hoarse. Heat burned my face. The air smelled of ash and dead trees.

"You did it," Allie said, but not as if she were glad.

I opened my eyes. Above I saw a molten blue sky, ahead of me an endless black plain. A few charred trunks jutted out of the dead land. Nothing else: just Matthew and me, Allie and Tallow beside her, Rebecca in her sling with her eyes scrunched closed and her head buried against my shoulder.

I staggered. The sky seemed so heavy, pressing like lead toward the earth. Matthew stood with me, not releasing his hold. Ash crunched beneath our feet. Water beaded on my jacket and Rebecca's sling and the backs of Matthew's and my hands, evaporating into the dry air. My hair was damp, too, as was Matthew's. Water droplets fell toward the earth but dried before they reached it.

Above, the sun shone like hammered copper. Tallow nudged Allie's hand, but she didn't move to scratch the cat's ears. She reached down and sifted a handful of ash through her wet fingers. The wind picked up, blowing the ash away and leaving black streaks on her hands and face. No bird flew. No animal called. No tree whispered to the wind. Faerie—yet I knew now Faerie hadn't always been like this.

"It's worse than Caleb told me," Allie whispered. "I had no idea." She looked down at her ash-stained hands. "The fey don't live forever, you know, no matter what people think. Harder to kill, harder to heal. That's what Caleb says."

The fey folk lost as much as we did during the War.

My people had done this. Ash blew into my eyes and clogged my throat. Whatever power had done this, it was better gone, along with the ways of making nylon and plastic and knives that kept their edge.

Behind me someone began to sing in a voice dry as old corn husks:

"Soft the drowsy hours are creeping,
Hill and vale in slumber sleeping,
All through the night ..."

I stiffened. Wind burned the dampness from my face. Slowly I turned, scarcely daring to breathe, knowing hope had no place in this dead land.

Behind me lay a small lake, a stone's throw across. Orange flames danced beneath its surface, as if the lake bottom was on fire. The lake was perfectly round and perfectly still. Less than a hundred paces away a figure huddled on the far bank, rocking back and forth as she sang. My throat felt dry, but that might have been from the heat.

I walked around to her, ignoring heat, ignoring wind, ignoring sky. Matthew and Allie and Tallow followed, but their steps seemed far away. Only the woman by the lake mattered. I knelt beside her and reached out slowly, afraid this was some vision that would dissolve at my touch.

"Mom." I said, and laid a hand on her shoulder.

Mom stared into the water and sang on, as if I hadn't spoken, as if I weren't there at all.

⁖ Chapter 14 ⁖

Flames rose from beneath the water and subsided again. Mom stretched her hands into the lake as if reaching for something. Her arms were red, burned—she didn't seem to notice. Her lips were cracked and bleeding. Red marks and ash streaked her face and neck. A pack lay open beside her, half-filled with black dust. I saw a canvas bag and a couple empty water bottles within.

Weight settled like lead in my stomach. Rebecca reached toward Mom, made an uncertain sound, and drew back.

I shook Mom's shoulder, first gently, then harder. She leaned away from me, her hair trailing into the lake. I bent around to meet her gaze. Her eyes were dull as ash.

"*Mom!*" I put force into that call, as much

force as I could. Mom sang on, unhearing. I thought I might throw up. Sweat trickled down my neck, evaporating before it could get beneath my sweater. I felt something cool against my skin and reached beneath the sweater to clutch Caleb's token. I took the chain from around my neck and offered it to Mom, praying there was some power in the disk.

For just a moment her eyes focused and her song fell silent. She grabbed the disk, jerking the chain from my hand. Then her gaze changed to something young and far away.

"Tara," Matthew whispered. His bare feet were black with ash. He rubbed at his scar as if it itched something fierce.

Allie reached tentatively out to touch Mom's cheek. "Something's wrong," the girl said. "I don't understand. She's lost, but not only lost. Something's wrong."

Mom's lips moved, forming words I couldn't hear. Around her neck her own disk hung, the veined metal bright in the sun.

"Mom." She had to answer. I'd make her answer.

She stared into the glowing water, as if she saw something I couldn't. Visions, I thought, but I didn't know whether the visions came from the lake or from somewhere inside her. I gripped her shoulder tighter. I remembered Caleb grabbing my arm, forcing my gaze to a mirror. He'd followed me.

I drew my hand abruptly away. I couldn't enter my mother's thoughts like Caleb had entered mine. I had no right.

But I also couldn't lose her. I couldn't let the darkness swallow her, not after I'd come so far. I turned to Matthew. "Be my watcher," I said.

Allie drew a sharp breath. "Mind injuries aren't like other hurts, Liza. You can't go in and heal this as if it were a break or a fever."

I forced my voice steady. "I'm not trying to heal it. I'm just trying to find her." I'd worry about healing later. I untied Rebecca's sling and set her down beside me. "Matthew?"

He looked first at Mom, then at me. "I'll watch you. I won't let you get lost."

No one could promise I wouldn't get lost, not when magic was involved.

"Trust me," Matthew said, and he gave a lopsided smile. I did trust him, whether it made sense to or not.

Tallow stalked to Rebecca's side as if keeping a watch of her own. Allie threw a handful of ash across the plain. "Be careful, Liza. I didn't heal you so you could get yourself killed some other way, you know."

"I know," I told her.

Mom still clutched Caleb's disk. I gently placed my hand over hers. Her skin was hot. I followed her gaze to the water. Flames roared up, and for a moment I felt I was falling through the fire. It burned all around me, and in the flames I saw —

Sun through leaves, a soft breeze swaying high branches. I walked without fear through a blue-green forest. No vines lashed out, no thorns tore at my boots. The mossy earth felt soft beneath my feet. A small bird flew past with a twig in its mouth, building a nest amid the leaves. Those leaves were perfectly round, bright with afternoon light. Or maybe the light came from within the leaves. I couldn't tell —

A young man and a young woman walked through the forest, their fingers interlaced, a hawk riding on the man's shoulder. Caleb again, and with him —

215

I'd seen her before, but I hadn't known her until now. How could she and Caleb — he should have been younger then, but who knew how long the faerie folk lived? I reached for the woman's hand. "Mom."

She drew back, turning to Caleb. "I don't understand," she said. To Caleb, not to me.

"It is time for you to return to your own people, Tara. Past time."

Mom shook her head. "No. There is nothing for me there. And if I return, my father will never let me out of his sight again."

"This isn't even real," Caleb said soberly. "This is past, this is memory. It cannot be undone." He drew his fingers from hers. "You must go. Our commanders have met, Karinna among them. War draws near, to your land and to mine."

Mom laughed, a joyless sound. "Most of my people don't even believe in your land. It's a ballad, a song, a story for children."

"But some of those who do believe hold power in your world, including your father. Just as some of those who disdain to talk to your people hold power in mine. Anger catches on all sides, like fire to fallen wood. The time when words could quench it is past."

Mom looked up as if to protest, but then Caleb

216

bent and brushed his lips against hers. I wanted to cry out, to tell him to leave her alone — but there was longing in her eyes as he drew away. Caleb took something from beneath his shirt: a silver disk on a chain, the disk Mom had worn all my life. If it weren't so clearly metal, it could have been a leaf fallen from one of the trees. Mom reached for it, then drew back her hand.

"Take it," Caleb said. "It's a gift to follow you from my world into yours." He draped the chain around her neck. "The quia leaf beneath the plating is real enough."

"I have little to offer in turn. I've always had less to offer." Mom fumbled in her pockets, pulled out a disk of her own. "Here."

Caleb turned it in his hands. An arch was inscribed on its surface, and a river, and words from Before. "I shall treasure it."

Mom laughed, a brittle sound like the crackle of old plastic. "It's just a quarter. Worth next to nothing in my world."

"I shall treasure it just the same."

"It's not so simple, you know. My world, your world. You're the one who told me that our worlds are linked by more than the Arch. There's less place for *me there than here."*

"There is no place for you here. I am sorry. If you still care for my world when the War is through, return then. The quia leaf will open the way to the land of its growth, even if none of my people are here to greet you. And should you choose not to return, still the leaf will protect you when you walk in dark forests."

"This parting is your choice, Kaylen, not mine." *Mom's shoulders stiffened as she turned from him. "If you wish to see me again when this is through, come into my world and find me."*

Caleb shut his eyes as if in pain. "All may yet be well. Goodbye, Tara."

Mom walked away, not crying, not looking back. I fell into step beside her and reached for her hand again. This time she let me take it. "Come on, Mom. We're going home." Mom shuddered at the word, but she followed me through the cool forest. The sun above us grew brighter. I shut my eyes against it, and when I opened them again —

I knelt with Mom beside the lake. Flames danced beneath its surface. Sun burned against my face. Mom's hand fell limp, and the quarter rolled to the ground. I stared at her, remembering a young woman, a stranger.

She turned to me, her eyes dull as old coals. "You should have left me there," she said.

I jerked as if slapped, even as Mom turned to the water once more.

I grabbed her arm, trying to pull her away. She fought me, and as she fought she started coughing, dry coughs that rasped through her chest like wind through old paper. I didn't care. I shook her harder. She'd run away; she'd left me; I wouldn't let her leave me. How could Mom abandon me for Faerie, for Caleb, for a stranger who wasn't even human? I felt hands trying to pull me away, but no one could make me let go. I began crying or screaming, I couldn't tell which. My chest and throat burned beneath the cursed Faerie sun.

As if in answer Rebecca cried out from where I'd set her down. Mom went limp in my arms. I went still, too. Only the wind blew on. "Rebecca?" Pain flashed through Mom's eyes like lightning. "No, you're Liza. Oh, God, Lizzy, I'm sorry, so sorry. I only sought a safe place for us all. I failed you ..." She stumbled to her feet, and I helped her up, but then her legs gave way.

I caught her and helped her back to the ground.

Matthew held a water bottle to her lips. I should have thought of that. I trembled like a leaf fighting wind. Perhaps Mom only needed water or food.

Mom took a swallow, coughed up water and phlegm and little spatters of blood. She closed her eyes, whimpering like a child. Matthew glanced at me, looking as lost as I felt. He opened his mouth as if to speak, but no words came out. He held the water out again. Mom shoved it away. The bottle flew from Matthew's hands and spilled to the ground. Ash swallowed water, leaving dry earth behind.

Allie moved to Mom's side, hesitant as a cat near fire. She moved slow healer's hands over Mom's body, then jerked back as if burned. I knew by the look on her face that this was more than dehydration or hunger.

"Allie?" I said.

Her hands shook, and she wouldn't meet my eyes. She looked at Matthew instead.

"It's like something's coming unraveled inside her. I don't understand. I need more time, but if I touch her too long—if I try to heal her—I'll start unraveling, too."

"Don't," Matthew said at once. Beneath the sun his face was ashy pale.

"We can't lose her," I said.

Allie's hands clenched and unclenched. "Don't ask me again, Liza. If you ask again, I won't be able to say no."

I bit my lip, swallowing my words. Wind blew through my silence.

Allie stood and backed away. "There's more. Whatever made her sick, I think it's still in the air here. I think if we stay too long, we'll get sick, too."

I brushed the hair back from my mother's forehead. Her skin burned beneath my touch. "Mom," I whispered. I wanted her to tell me everything would be all right, but she closed her eyes and said nothing.

In a small voice Allie asked, "How do we leave this place, Liza?"

There was no Arch here, no way out. There was only dust and heat and ashes.

Matthew looked down at Mom, then up at

me, and I saw despair in his eyes. But he only said, "Through the lake again, right?"

I nearly asked what he meant, but then I remembered my vision of Caleb stepping into burning water. I thought about how the water hadn't burned or drowned him. He hadn't died, not unless it was the future I'd seen.

I ran a hand through my hair. It was stiff—wind and heat had dried the water in it. I remembered the water on my jacket and on Tallow's fur. Of course we'd come through the lake. We had to step into this world from some-where. Lost in the visions that had brought us here, I hadn't seen—but the way through had two sides. The Arch in my world. The lake in this one.

Fire flared through the lake's surface, bright against the blue sky. Tallow batted a pebble. Her paws were covered with soot. So were my hands and the legs of my pants. The fire receded, and the lake was still. Still as the drawn water in which my magic had first found me. Running water held little magic, but still water was like metal, like glass, like a mirror.

Yet if we stepped through the lake, emerging

safely through the Arch on the other side — what then? It would be four or five days to Washville. Along the way we'd have to resist the River and hold back the shadows all over again, all while dragging or carrying Mom with us.

"How much time do we — does Mom — have?" I asked Allie.

Allie's face scrunched up, but her voice held steady. "No one can know that for sure, Liza. Caleb always says so."

I forced myself not to flinch from the truth I heard there. "But you don't think it's very long."

Allie turned and grabbed Tallow in her arms. The cat squirmed, but Allie didn't let go.

Matthew reached for my hand. Mom began coughing again. I thought of how she'd stepped through the Arch, trusting Caleb's quia leaf to see her through, not knowing that she might die on the other side.

Or maybe she had known. *You should have left me there.* Maybe she'd known all along.

"The War was stupid," Allie said. "So stupid."

I thought of the Arch, reaching like a mirror

toward the sky. I thought of Mom, and the young woman Mom had once been, both stepping through.

"A mirror." My hand had passed through Caleb's mirror easily enough, but it had been too small to let anything but my hand through. "Will any mirror big enough do?"

Still not looking at me, Allie said, "It's your magic. You'd know better than us."

I glanced at Matthew. His eyes went wide. "Gram's mirror," he said.

I nodded. Kate's mirror was taller than any of us. "Gram said the mirror was a family heirloom, that she couldn't bear to destroy it during the War," Matthew said. "Do you think it would work, Liza? Gram doesn't have any magic, but she does understand about healing. She might know what to do."

Allie dropped Tallow and gazed into the water. "It looks deep." She stepped back, shivering in spite of the heat.

"I know," I said, thinking that Allie and I both knew too much about drowning. "If my magic fails —"

The girl whirled to face me, her expression fierce. "But if we stay here we'll die for sure."

"That makes it easy, then." I tried to laugh, but the sound came out strangled and strange.

Mom's coughing quieted. She didn't struggle as Matthew and I helped her to her feet, but she didn't look at us, either. Sun glinted off Caleb's quarter. I picked up the necklace and draped it around my own neck again. I left Mom leaning on Matthew and tied Rebecca's sling around my neck. Rebecca whimpered. Mom strained toward the sound. "Rebecca. Lizzy. My babies, my girls ..."

I took Mom's hand. Matthew kept supporting her from the other side. Allie set Tallow on her shoulders, then reached for Matthew in turn. She clutched his hand as tightly as she'd clutched the guide ropes over the river. Matthew turned to me. His face and hair were soot-darkened, his eyes puffy, as if he wanted to cry but didn't dare. Yet somehow he managed to smile — as if saying without words that he trusted me still, as much as I trusted him.

I drew a breath and looked into the burning lake, seeking visions to guide us home.

❧ Chapter 15 ❧

The visions didn't come.

Hesitantly I stepped into the water, my eyes on the flames beneath its surface. The water didn't burn. It flowed over my boots, warm but not hot. Light reflected from the sun above the water and the flames below. I took another step, and in the lake's light I saw — but then flames erupted near my elbow, and the vision vanished. I jerked my arm back, ignoring the stench of charred wool. Rebecca cried softly. Mom stumbled, trying to pull free of my grasp. I tightened my grip and looked into the lake once more. Somehow I knew that this water — that any water — was different from metal or glass, harder to see in and harder to control.

I looked into the lake and pictured Kate's

mirror: its gold frame, its silvered glass. I pictured my own perfect reflection staring back at me. The water grew brighter. I stared into the brightness and saw —

Mom — the young woman who became Mom — kneeling in a green forest beside a blue lake, playing a flute. Caleb walked up behind her, and Karin as well, and they added their voices to the music —

Mom's hand tightened in mine, and I knew that we saw together once more.

Saw Mom running amid a ragged stream of refugees, fleeing a city that burned and crumbled behind her —

Mom at the edge of our town, her eyes cast downward as Father and Jayce tried to turn her away. But Kate stood there, too, saying, "She's little more than a child. For pity's sake, let her stay — "

Father, holding Mom close, whispering, "I will keep you safe." They were both older, but not a lot older —

Water rose past my waist. I clung to Mom's hand. Kate's mirror, I thought. I held my gaze steady, and I saw —

Mom and Kate staring at the ruins of a burned house while Kate whispered, "Cam's not the only one, Tara. I need your help — "

Mom and Kate watching as Matthew growled and shifted in his sleep, as Stefan and Emma's son called corn husks through the air to his outstretched hand, as Jayce's granddaughter set dry wood aflame at a glance. "Stay hidden," Mom warned each of them in turn. "Stay safe —"

Mom frowning as Father led me out to hunt with bow and arrow, but turning away when Kyle, Brianna's youngest, tugged on her sleeve. "I can talk to ants," the boy said. "Want to see?"

Mom's frown deepened. She put a finger to her lips. "Don't tell," she said.

"Course not," Kyle answered. "We don't tell anyone but you and Kate. Every kid knows that —"

Every kid but me. While Father had taught me to hunt, Mom had taught the other children how to hide their magic. And when she left, she'd spoken to Kate — but not me. Never me.

Mom's hand slipped from my grasp. I grabbed it again. "Not this time," I said. "You're not leaving me this time." I held on as water soaked through my sweater. The vision nearly slid away, but somehow I caught it once more and saw —

Kate standing at the foot of Mom's bed, her expression fierce. "Let it go," Kate said. "Even if you could find your way back to Faerie, even if anyone survived there — and you know how unlikely that is, given the weapons we used — they wouldn't welcome you."

Mom sat up in bed. Her face was drawn and pale, her hair unbrushed. "They won't turn the children away, not once they know about their magic. Don't you see, Kate? Rebecca won't be the last, any more than Cam was. The children aren't safe here anymore. We have to find someplace else for them."

"What about your other daughter?" Kate demanded. "Will you leave her here to wonder where you've gone?"

Mom shut her eyes. "You know I can't tell Liza. If she let anything slip to Ian — no. He'd kill them all. I just give thanks she doesn't have any magic of her own. We could never keep that from Ian. I'm protecting her, too."

Kate's mouth twisted into an angry frown. "If you want to protect her, take her with you. Take her away from him."

Mom shook her head and turned away. Instead I saw —

Father walking down the stairs, a bundle in his arms. I watched from my room, silent as a shadow, *knowing there was nothing I could do —*

Water rose around me. The weight of the sling dug into my neck. An icy hand touched my cheek. I had to do something —

I ran after Father, into the hall, down the stairs. But even as I ran I knew I was too late —

"You're late, Liza." Father turned to me, belt in hand. I wanted to make him go away, like I'd made the trees go away, but words stuck in my throat. I was weak, just like he said. Too weak to fight him, too weak to run. The belt came down on my back. I fell to my knees, fighting not to cry out. If I cried out I would drown, and if I drowned I would never find —

Find what? Father's belt broke skin as I struggled to think. The sling grew heavier, filling with water. They were all depending on me, trusting me —

I stood, forcing my head above water.

Father froze with his belt in midair. I walked past him, away from him: across the room and out the door. My back ached, but I wasn't so weak that I couldn't do what needed to be done. I walked through the town, slow as if moving through water, but I walked. I opened Kate's door, crossed her living room, and drew her wall hangings aside. The mirror stood there. I kept walking, toward the silvered glass —

Dizziness overtook me. There was a sound like water crashing to shore, and a moment's darkness —

And then I stepped out of Kate's mirror, coughing up water, my hair and clothes dripping, Rebecca wailing in her sling. Kate looked up from her loom, her eyes wide with astonishment. My hand, still half in the mirror, clutched Mom's. I tried to pull her after me, but Mom pulled back, away. For an instant I saw dark waters, and I knew Mom sought their depths. "Not this time," I said again. Then, louder, *"Mom. Tara. Come here."* Mom stumbled through the glass, shivering violently. Matthew stepped after her, then Allie and Tallow.

Mom's smile was bitter. "You're not going to let me go, are you?"

"No."

She sighed and crumpled to the floor, even as Kate rushed to her side. Rebecca's cries slowed to gulping sobs.

"Tara," Kate said.

Mom looked up. "You told me I was a fool,"

she whispered to Kate, and shut her eyes.

Kate knelt by Mom's side. If she felt any pain in her knees, she ignored it. She checked Mom's pulse and breathing, examined the burn marks, and laid a hand on her forehead. "Matthew," she said, her face tight, "a bucket of cold water and some towels."

Matthew dropped the pack and ran from the room. I clutched Mom's hand. Her skin was so hot.

"I'm a healer," Allie said. "I can help."

Kate nodded. "Tell me her symptoms. Except for the fever. I've figured that out."

Allie told Kate everything. Kate blinked once when Allie described her magical probing, but she kept listening. The way she looked at Mom made my stomach twist.

Matthew returned with the water. Kate dipped a towel into the bucket and pressed it against Mom's forehead. "This is important," she said. "I need to know exactly where you've been."

Allie looked up. "It was the air, wasn't it? I knew there was something in the air. I could feel it."

"Where?" Kate asked, tension clear in her voice.

"Faerie," I said.

"How long?"

"We don't know how long for Mom."

"And for the rest of you?"

"An hour," I said. "Maybe two."

Kate nodded. The tension eased a little, but then she lifted her hands from the towel and buried her face in them. "I don't suppose you're familiar with the term 'radiation poisoning'? No, of course not." She stood, leaving the towel on Mom's forehead. "I want all of you out of those clothes and scrubbed down, every square inch of skin, every last bit of ash. Especially the baby." The sling covered Rebecca's face. As Kate spoke she reached out and drew it back. She froze. "Rebecca?" she whispered.

"I was too late." My voice was flat.

Kate pressed her lips together. "We were all too late, one way or another." She pulled me into a swift hug, held Matthew a moment as well. "Seeing both of you back safely is already more than I'd hoped for. Now out of those clothes. The effects of radiation have a lot to do with the length of exposure, and your clothes can hold particles you can't see."

"I'm always too late." I didn't release Mom's hand.

"Liza." The anger in Kate's voice startled me. "Don't you *dare* go blaming yourself for this." She drew me roughly to my feet and turned me to face her. "This began before you were born. You did all anyone could expect and more. Now get out of those things. You can wash in the kitchen. I'll stay with your mother, and when you're through we'll wash her, too."

I sighed, brushing a stray hair from Mom's face, even as Kate hugged Matthew again, then Allie. "I'm sorry," I told Mom, then stood and followed Matthew and Allie from the room.

The well was working again. Allie and I filled buckets and carried them in. Outside the sun was low, and the chill air raised goose bumps beneath my wet sweater and jacket. Soon oaks and maples and sycamores would shiver with cold, shaking winter snows from their green leaves.

Matthew met us in the kitchen with soap and

towels and changes of clothes from upstairs. I bent to pull off my boots, then hesitated. I glanced uncomfortably at Matthew. He glanced uncomfortably back, and his neck flushed red.

"Come on," Allie said. She already had her jacket and boots off and was tugging on her socks.

"Um," I said, even as I thought how I'd seen Matthew without clothes before, how it shouldn't matter.

"I'll go see if Gram needs any help," Matthew said quickly. "I'll come back when you're through."

Allie rolled her eyes as he left. "Boys are silly, you know that?"

I didn't answer.

We scrubbed down hard with the cold water, shivering all the while. It took both of us to wash Tallow. When we finished, the old cat shook herself and stalked indignantly away. We put our ash-coated clothes into a plastic bin and changed into clean ones. Matthew had also brought a blanket for a new sling. When I wrapped Rebecca in it she looked up at me and smiled, a quiet baby smile that was free of tears. My heart tightened in my chest. She would never be more than shadow.

Allie rolled her pants and sleeves up. Our feet were bare. We'd have to find or make new boots later. I hesitated, then hung Caleb's disk around my neck once more. Allie tried to braid her tangled hair, but quickly gave up and let it fall loose like mine.

"Maybe things will be all right after all," she said hopefully, and followed me toward the kitchen doorway.

From the living room I heard Kate's voice.

"I've never wished so hard for a perfectly ordinary emergency room, or a phone that could dial nine-one-one. But I doubt even that would help her." Kate sounded tired and old. "Truth is, Matthew, there's not much any of us can do. Keep her comfortable. Give her what we can for the pain."

"Liza," Allie breathed. She grabbed my hand so tightly my fingers hurt.

"Before it would have been different," Kate said. "There was always something more we could try Before."

My stomach knotted. I crept forward and peered through the doorway. Kate had propped Mom up on some pillows. The ash had been scrubbed from her skin, and beneath the blankets she wore only a loose nightshirt. Matthew slowly poured water from a cup down her throat. Mom didn't move, not even to take the cup from his hands.

"I can call her back." My words were high and strange. "As often as I have to."

"That won't make her well," Allie said. She kept holding my hand.

I looked down at Rebecca. The baby breathed softly in her new sling, as if asleep. "I don't care. I'll do it anyway."

Matthew looked up and saw us. He handed the cup to Kate and headed toward the kitchen, his shoulders hunched. He didn't speak as he walked past us toward the buckets and soap.

"I hate this," Allie said. "Hate it, hate it, hate it!" And then, "I wish Caleb were here. He'd know what to do. He'd know how to heal this, or whether it really was too late. He'd know."

I bit back a sharp retort. I wished Caleb were here, too.

"How far apart do you think our towns are, Liza? Maybe we can get him. Maybe if we leave right away—"

"A day apart," I said, remembering the map and thinking how we'd have to get there and back both.

"Oh," Allie said in a small voice, and I knew that was too far. "It's not fair!" she shouted. Kate looked toward us. "I wish Caleb wasn't so far away. I wish you could just call and make him come!"

"Allie!" My heart started pounding. "Maybe I can."

I bolted across the living room, knowing better than to hope, hoping anyway.

"What is it, child?" Kate asked, but I ran past her, to the mirror.

Swiftly I untied the sling and set it down beside me. In the glass my hair was streaked pale, but I didn't care. I grabbed Caleb's quarter in both hands as I looked into the mirror. "*Caleb!*" He was too far away to call by voice alone, but maybe in visions I could find him. Mom had seen me, after all, through glass and through water. Maybe Caleb would see me, too. Maybe the time we saved, if he answered my call, would be enough.

The mirror turned to silver, my reflection fading into the brightness. I kept staring, kept calling until I saw —

Caleb and Karin walking through our ruined city, the Arch growing small behind them, grief clear enough on both their faces. Karin leaned on Caleb as if she'd been hurt, though there was no wound that I could see —

Caleb guiding Allie's hands over a goat's wounded leg. Allie laughing as the leg mended. Caleb smiling, a different smile than Before, older and sadder, for all that his face remained young —

I pushed through the visions. They were in the past, and I needed the present. "Caleb!"

Samuel and Caleb hunched over a late-afternoon fire. A small pot sat on the coals. Samuel stared silently into the distance, while Caleb's face was grim and hard as stone.

They weren't in Washville. Of course they weren't. They'd gone out looking for Allie.

"*Caleb!*" I called, even as I wondered—why hadn't Father gone looking for me?

Caleb reached out to pour something into the pot. His glance caught on its metal surface, and his hand froze in midair. He looked right at me and opened his mouth as if to speak—

I heard footsteps behind me. Caleb faded away, and in the bright mirror I saw—

Father approaching one slow step at a time. With a sick lurch I knew this was no vision. I watched him, knowing better, always knowing better than to run.

Father's hand came down on my shoulder. He turned me firmly about.

"Liza," he said, and his voice was hard as metal that refused to give way, "where have you been?"

❧ Chapter 16 ❧

Words froze in my throat as I stared up at my father. Maybe I needed only to explain. Maybe once he understood —

"Have you grown too stupid to speak?"

Kate stood and moved to my side. "Let her be, Ian."

"Stay out of this. I asked my daughter a question."

"M-mom," I managed to stammer. "Mom was ill. We found her, and we brought her here — "

Father slapped me. I staggered back. "I can see that much! Tell me how it happened. Tell me where you've both been."

My throat tightened. I hated the way my words came out, my voice close to breaking. "I

242

went looking for her after she left." That was close enough to truth. I didn't know whether he'd guessed at the magic in Kate's mirror — though surely he could see my hair if nothing else — but the rage in his face was enough to tell me I still didn't want to talk to him about magic, no matter whom it healed or failed to heal. "I went looking, and I found her, and I brought her home." That much I'd done right, at least. I'd brought Mom home. Surely even Father could see that.

"She knew the rules," he said. "You knew the rules. Why did you break them? Why did you venture out alone into the dark?"

Because I'd feared if I stayed, I'd do harm — but I knew that would be the wrong answer, too. Father drew his hand back again.

"Ian!" Kate stepped between us. "You leave her alone. You get out of my house."

Father shoved her aside, his eyes never leaving me. Kate fell to the floor with a cry as Father grabbed my shoulders. "Answer me!" He started shaking me. From the corner of my eye I saw Allie grab a branch from the firewood pile, like a weapon. If I could have spoken at all, I'd have told her to run away. She was a stranger. He'd hurt her worse than he'd hurt me.

Father shook me harder, his face red with rage. My shoulders hurt, and my breath came out in gasps. I couldn't have answered him if I tried. I fell to my knees, and he reached for his belt.

Matthew stepped through the kitchen doorway, taking the room in at a glance. Fury darkened his features. Matthew never got angry, I thought numbly, but I knew better. He ran at Father, changing as he did, arms lengthening into legs, face into snout, fur flowing like melting silver over his skin. Even as Matthew leaped Father whirled around, throwing an arm in front of his throat, putting his body between me and the wolf.

Matthew sank his teeth into Father's arm. Father's face twisted in pain, but he held his ground, reaching for his knife with his free hand. Matthew's teeth sank deeper, snapping bone, drawing blood through Father's sleeve. I remembered Matthew's rage as he'd lain half-conscious under Caleb's care. *I'll tear him limb from limb.* Matthew would kill Father, I realized with a sick, cold feeling. I struggled to my feet.

Without warning Father threw his weight forward, knocking Matthew onto his back and shoving a knee into his chest. I heard ribs crack. Fur swiftly receded, leaving a human boy behind. Father didn't even hesitate, he just drew his knife toward Matthew's throat. "At least Cam was too young to know better," he growled.

"*Father!*" I put all the command I could into that call. It was the same call I'd used to bring Allie back from the river, to bring Mom back from Faerie. "*Father, stop!*"

His blade halted against Matthew's skin. Matthew glared at him, eyes hot with rage, a wolf's eyes still.

I didn't dare let my gaze, my command, waver. "*Father, come here.*"

Slowly, fighting the compulsion all the way, Father stood, grasping the knife in one hand. His other arm hung strangely at his side. Slower yet, he turned to face me. Clutching her branch uncertainly, Allie moved behind him. Tallow crouched behind Allie's legs, hissing.

"What witchery is this, Liza?"

"*Give me the knife,*" I commanded, holding out my hand, calling the knife to me.

His arm trembled, but he reached forward and handed it to me. His eyes flicked to my hair as if seeing it — as if seeing me — for the first time. "Not you, Liza. This taint of magic cannot have touched you."

I spoke slowly, holding my control, not trusting him. Had I ever trusted him? "Magic isn't what you think." Treacherous hope rose in me. Maybe he truly didn't understand, like I hadn't understood. "Magic doesn't always kill."

Father's eyes didn't leave me. "What can you possibly understand about magic? You weren't there during the War. You have no idea what magic can do."

I'd seen as much of the War as he had, now. And I did understand, maybe for the first time. "Magic is a tool, like a knife or a bow. We can learn how to wield it." I thought of Cam, and I knew no tool is ever fully safe, but we could learn to use this one. We had to learn, if we were going to survive.

Father spat, and I knew doing even that much

while I held him took great effort. His knife felt heavy in my hand. "That's your mother talking, Liza, not you. I should have known your mother was magic-cursed the moment she came to this town, knowing no one, playing at innocence. But she had me fooled well enough, right until she bore that monster. Then I knew. She knew, too, or else why would she have gone? She should have done us a favor and gone sooner."

I listened, frozen by the quiet hate in his words, wondering who held whom.

"But you, Liza. You're not like her. You know what needs doing, and you're not afraid to do it." He still couldn't move, but his gaze flicked to the blade. His voice took on a strange, hard pity. "Give me the knife, Liza. I swear to you there won't be any pain."

That pity told me, more than any anger, that he'd never understand. Still I tried one more time. "Magic can heal. I've seen it."

"Magic kills," Father said.

"No," Allie squeaked from behind him. "Liza's right. Look " She dropped the branch and reached for his injured arm. I saw silver light and knew bones were knitting back together.

Father jerked away as if burned, my hold on him lost. He whirled and grabbed Allie by her shirt. I flung myself between them, even as Tallow yowled and leaped at Father's face. The cat's claws dug into his skin. Father cursed as he fought to pull Tallow away one-handed. He grabbed her by the scruff of the neck and hurled her across the room. She gave a single startled mew, then hit the wall with a *thud* and fell motionless to the ground. In her sling on the floor, Rebecca began to cry.

Father froze at the sound. We all did. For an endless moment Father stared at the sling, Rebecca's shadow face just visible within its folds. Then, rage in every step, he stalked to where she lay.

Something crossed his face—regret, sorrow, maybe love. It quickly faded, replaced by something fiercer. He looked toward where Mom lay, her eyes closed, her skin flushed with fever.

"You couldn't let her go, could you, Tara?"

Mom shuddered at his words but didn't

open her eyes.

"We'll put an end to this right now." Father reached for Rebecca's sling. She screamed, an animal sound I'd never heard from any human child. I dropped Father's knife and threw myself over my sister, not caring that she was only shadow, knowing only that I wouldn't let him touch her ever again.

"Liza," he said, "this needs to be done."

I looked up at him, clutching Rebecca in my arms. So cold — but I could handle the cold. I could handle lots of things.

"This is some witchery of your mother's, nothing more. Let her go."

I shook my head. "Mom didn't call Rebecca back. I did." I stood, still holding Rebecca, and faced him. He was taller than me, but not as tall as I'd remembered. "This is my magic," I told him. "Only mine."

Father's face twisted for a moment into something like grief. Then it was gone, and he lunged for the knife I'd left on the floor. I kicked it out of his reach. Allie grabbed the knife, even as Rebecca's screams quieted to gulping sobs.

"Father," I said.

His face held no grief now, only rage. He stood, glaring all the while. My anger rose to meet his. So many years I'd tried to be good enough, to be strong enough. They meant nothing to him, nothing at all. Ashes and dust. That was all the War had left any of us.

"*Go,*" I told him, feeling power and command grow within me. If I could call things to me, I could also send them away. I could send Father away, as far away as I wanted. He stumbled back, his injured arm held to one side, his face growing pale.

"*Go.*" As far as the place I'd called Allie back from, that was how far I could send him. For the first time I saw fear cross Father's face. It felt good, having him be the one who was afraid. A few more words, a bit more magic, and he would never trouble me again. "*Go.*" Father's hand moved to his chest, as at some pain.

"Liza," Matthew whispered. He still lay on the floor, wincing at pain of his own. He didn't try to stop me, but he looked afraid as well. Afraid of me.

You're not like him, Matthew had said, but what if I was? What if we all were? I thought of trees grinding flesh into dust. I thought of fire falling from a hot blue sky. People—faerie or human— had commanded the trees, and the fire as well.

I thought of Father's blade at Matthew's throat. I thought of bones on a hillside. If I killed him, he wouldn't be able to harm anyone ever again. Killing him only made sense.

The War had likely made sense, too, once, if it came down to that.

Rebecca felt so cold in my arms. I fought not to shiver. Father was a sensible man. If he had been in my place, I'd have already been dead.

"*Go.*" My voice shook, but there was power behind my words. "*Walk away from this town. Go as far and as fast as you can, and never trouble those who live here again.*"

The fear in Father's eyes gave way to anger once more. His whole body trembled as he struggled against my command. "I saved this town. Every person in it would have died if not for me."

"You saved us," I agreed. "But that was before. The War is over. *Go*."

Father met my steady gaze with his own. "This town will die without me. Wait and see."

He stalked away without another word, across the room and out the door. I followed to the doorway. Townsfolk coming in from the fields stopped by their houses and watched him leave. Not one of them tried to stop him.

But they hadn't tried to stop any of the things he'd done, either.

I kept staring until Father disappeared from view, beyond the town and into the forest. "Go away," I whispered, feeling very young. "Go away, go away, go away."

The shadow in my arms sobbed on. I turned back to see Allie carefully setting Father's knife down by the woodpile. She looked around her, from Kate to Matthew to Tallow, as if not sure what to do next. She started toward Matthew, but he shook his head. "Gram first. Ribs heal, even without magic." Allie nodded and moved to Kate's side.

"Rebecca." Mom sat up slowly, painfully. She

looked at me, her eyes suddenly clear. Rebecca fell silent. Mom held out her arms like a child waiting for a gift.

I brushed a finger along Rebecca's cold cheek. What magic would she have had, had she grown? I'd never know. I unwrapped the sling and held my sister close, not caring how deep the cold burned. "I'm sorry," I told her. "I'd bring you back if I could." But some things really were beyond magic's power to heal. I knelt by Mom's side and placed the shadow into her arms.

Rebecca gurgled, all sign of tears gone. A sad smile crossed Mom's face. "Rebecca," she whispered. She stroked the baby's shadow hair and sang,

"I my loving vigil keeping,
All through the night."

The shadow sank deep into Mom's arms, past skin and bone. I heard a sound like a baby's laughter, and then Rebecca was gone, leaving only Mom's singing as she drew her arms around herself. After a time the singing stopped, too, and Mom sank back to the pillows. When I felt her forehead, it was cool.

She reached out and gripped my hands in her own. "All may yet be well," she whispered, and then she shut her eyes once more.

❧ Chapter 17 ❧

My arms felt empty without Rebecca to hold. I longed to call her back, but I forced the longing down and away. The time for that was gone.

Ashes. Dust. Bones cracked in the moonlight.

For a time I remained by Mom's side, holding her cool hand, watching her chest rise and fall. Allie mended the broken bones in Kate's hip and leg, then examined Matthew. I scanned the room and found Tallow lying against the wall where Father had thrown her. The cat was still, eyes open and staring, fur yet damp from her bath.

"Tallow," I whispered. She didn't move. I remembered how I'd called her in the night once before. I'd been surprised when the old cat came to me then. Only now did I realize I must have called her with my magic, just like I'd called Allie.

"*Tallow,*" I called again, louder, but the cat didn't stir. Maybe she didn't want to come back this time. Maybe if I kept calling she'd come whether she wanted to or not.

The healer can't decide alone. I took Tallow in my arms, scratched her behind the ears, and said nothing at all.

Matthew shifted to wolf as Allie healed him, then shifted back when she was through. He went to the kitchen to dress, and Allie stumbled over to me. Her eyes were shadowed with lack of sleep and something more. Her gaze flicked to Tallow, but she didn't cry. She simply found a piece of old cloth by Kate's loom and silently handed it to me.

I wrapped Tallow up and set her down in Kate's battered old armchair. "It's not a feather bed," I whispered, my own eyes stinging, "but it'll have to do." Later I would bury her.

In a thin voice Allie said, "I think I'd better rest. I think I pushed too hard."

Kate tried to lead Allie to the stairs, but the girl shook her head. "Too far." She curled up on the couch instead, looking over at me wearily. "Liza, was that ..." She yawned, tried again.

"Was that your father?"

I nodded. Allie scrunched up her face. "I don't understand," she said. "So many things I don't ..." But then she yawned again, and shut her eyes, and fell asleep. She seemed suddenly young, curled up there.

Kate brushed a lock of tangled red hair from her face. "That girl's a wonder," she said.

Allie drew her arms around herself, called for Tallow, and began sobbing in her sleep. I swallowed hard, returned to Kate's mirror, and tried to call Caleb again.

The mirror filled with visions: of Caleb, of Mom, of myself on the road with Matthew and Allie. But those were all in the past. I couldn't find the present. Maybe Caleb also needed to be near glass or metal or water. Or maybe the failure was entirely my own. There was no way to know. In the end I returned to Mom's side and took her hand once more. I could see that her breathing had slowed, and I knew that cooling her fever hadn't been enough.

Kate, Matthew, and I stayed with Mom through the night, barely speaking. After a time, Matthew put his hand in mine. I held on as tightly as when he'd pulled me from the river, the night I'd left Franklin Falls.

The townspeople came to visit us, alone and in pairs. At first they came to ask about Father's leaving, but once they knew Mom was there, they came to visit her as well. The adults murmured quiet, awkward words. The children were mostly silent, keeping their magic hidden still, just as Mom had taught them.

Jayce the blacksmith surprised me by laying a hand on my shoulder and saying in his husky voice, "We should have sent Ian packing years ago. Thank you, Liza, for finding the courage we lacked."

No one seemed to regret Father's going. I tried, but I didn't regret it, either. Yet still I felt strange and empty inside. Like Father had left some cold, numb space behind, and I wasn't sure what to fill it with, or whether it could be filled.

* * *

When Allie woke the next morning she scrounged dried meat from Kate's kitchen and insisted we eat. I tried, but my stomach clenched after only a few bites, and I set the food aside.

Allie reached for Mom. I grabbed her hands in my own, stopping her, not wanting to stop her. Allie swallowed, nodded, and let her hands fall to her lap. Mom's chest continued to rise and fall. Nothing mattered but the next breath, and the next. "You shouldn't have gone," I whispered, knowing Mom couldn't hear.

Kate said, "Grief is a complicated thing. She did what she thought needed to be done."

"Alone," I said. "Because she didn't trust me." Even now, the words stung.

Kate stroked my hair. "She was scared, Liza. She wanted nothing more to do with magic, only I asked for her help. At first I only guessed she'd been to Faerie—a desperate guess, because I so badly needed someone who understood magic. Tara insisted she didn't really understand, but she knew more than she thought. She taught us about control and having watchers. She made sure the children never forgot they were human. But she was always terrified your father would find out. She thought she was protecting you by making sure you didn't know."

I drew my arms around myself. In the end, she hadn't protected me from anything.

The door creaked open behind us. Kate stood and I waited, expecting more townsfolk.

"Daddy," Allie squeaked. I turned then. Allie threw herself across the room so hard and fast she nearly knocked Samuel over. He held her as she burst into gulping sobs. There were circles under his eyes, and his hair stood on end, and he looked at Allie as if he didn't believe he really held her, as if he feared she'd disappear if he dared look away. I knew by that look that nothing mattered to him as much as the girl in his arms.

Had my father ever held me like that? I couldn't remember.

Beside him Caleb said slowly, "We thought you were dead. When we saw the rockslide and the light and the scraps that were all we could find of your backpacks." Unlike Samuel, Caleb's face and voice held no expression. "We thought you were dead, and we thought your town should know."

I stood and met his gaze, not caring what he

saw. "My mother is dying." My throat tightened around the words. "Can you save her?"

Caleb looked past me, and his face grew more impassive yet, like stone. He strode across the room to where Mom lay. I knelt by his side.

He ran his hands along her body, a series of short feather touches, none lingering too long.

"I couldn't heal her," Allie said in a small voice. Samuel still held her. "I tried, but I couldn't—I mean not without ..."

Caleb turned to her. "You did well," he said, and for an instant his expression softened. "I am glad you did not attempt more."

"But *you* can heal her, can't you?" Allie asked. I didn't dare speak, for fear of his answer.

"By the powers that be I'm going to try."

"Right, then." Allie squared her shoulders, pulled away from her father, and moved to Caleb's side.

Caleb shook his head. "Not this time, Allison. This I have to do alone."

"You'll go too far if I'm not here. You know you will."

Caleb set his hands gently on Allie's shoulders. "You are as gifted a healer as any faerieborn I had the honor to teach Before," he said. "But as your teacher I tell you that you are not ready for this."

"At least let me be your watcher."

Caleb cast an unreadable look my way. "Liza will watch."

"But why—"

"Trust me, Allison."

Allie drew a breath. "You'll make him be careful, won't you, Liza? You'll make sure he doesn't go too far?"

"I promise," I said, but my thoughts were with Mom, hoping, not daring to hope, there was something Caleb could do.

"I'll stay, too," Matthew said.

Caleb shook his head. "Only Liza." There was something in his voice—I still didn't trust him, not completely. But whatever the risk, I would take it.

Matthew reached for my hand again. His grip felt cool in mine. "Call if you need me. I'll be right outside." He squeezed my hand, then left. Kate and Samuel and Allie followed him, leaving me alone with Caleb and Mom.

Caleb brushed the hair back from Mom's forehead and gently traced the plated quia leaf she wore. Something slipped in his face, letting grief through. "You were right, Tara. I never should have forced you to leave again. The mistake was mine. I know that now."

Caleb turned to me, and his face hardened again, reminding me of the man who'd held me to a mirror. I didn't look away from him, though.

"Two things," he said, his voice hard as his gaze. "First: an apology. I had no right to force visions on you, or to enter your thoughts to see where the visions led. There were other ways, and I should have remembered them. I ask that you forgive me."

I said nothing. What was done was done. Like the War—it remained there behind us, whatever words we spoke or didn't speak. After a long moment, Caleb went on. "Second: once I start this healing, you are not to stop me. No matter what happens. Do you understand?"

I understood far too well. I thought how I'd

promised Allie, and shame burned my cheeks, but I remained silent.

Caleb nodded, taking my silence for the answer it was. "At least the fever's gone. That's a help." He placed his hands on Mom's chest. For a moment, two moments, his expression remained calm. Then his face tightened as if in pain. Mom bolted upright, screaming.

My heart pounded so hard I thought it'd burst from my chest. Caleb forced Mom back to the pillows, light flowing like water from his hands. Light flowed over Mom's chest and abdomen, her arms and legs. Her screams gave way to whimpers as she fought Caleb. Her eyes opened wide, but whatever she saw, it wasn't us. She struggled on. I couldn't breathe. I couldn't look away. Caleb's fingers dug into Mom's shoulders. She lurched up again and heaved violently, spewing blood and vomit on her clothes and his. When she fell back to the pillows, I rolled her to her side, even as Caleb fell beside her.

He pulled himself up with visible effort and put his hands to either side of her face. "Tara," he whispered, and I couldn't tell whether the name was a call or a prayer.

Mom opened her eyes, and tears spilled down her cheeks. Caleb traced a track through them with one finger, then sighed and sank to the floor, his lips twisting into a smile.

Mom sat up and looked at me, her eyes clear and focused, seeing me at last. "Liza," she whispered, as if in pain still. "Lizzy, my baby, my girl." She pulled me into a fierce hug.

I thought of all she'd hidden, of all she hadn't trusted me to know. I thought of how I'd found her and how she hadn't wanted to be found. But I hugged her back, drawing shuddering breaths, clinging like a child.

It took me several heartbeats to realize how silent Caleb was, several more to draw away from Mom. I put a hand to his neck. The skin was warm but I felt no pulse.

"Caleb," I called. No answer. I turned the word to a command. "*Caleb. Kaylen.*" Still nothing.

My throat went dry. *I promised Allie,* I thought again.

Mom reached out as if to shake him, then drew away, pain settling more deeply over her features. I'd been willing to accept what Caleb asked, but what about Mom? What about Allie?

Caleb's silver eyes were still open. I looked into them, seeing again how like mirrors they really were.

How far was too far? How long until you had no choice but to let someone go?

Caleb's eyes grew brighter, bright as metal, bright as moonlight. I didn't look away. I stared into those eyes, and as I stared I saw —

Caleb kneeling beneath a gray sky, sifting dark soil through his hands. Around him blackened trees rose like bones from the dead land.

I stood in that same land, saw those same trees. "Caleb," I called. He didn't hear. I walked toward him, and my legs were lead, almost too heavy to lift. Cinders crunched beneath my feet. Above a pale sun shone, giving no heat.

My skin was pale, too. My clothes were washed of all color. I knew I was here in mind only, that back in Kate's house my body slumped motionless as Caleb's. I called his name again. I tried to walk faster but I couldn't. I could only take one step, and the next, and the next. I reached out to touch Caleb's shoulder. He looked up, and there was no surprise, no grief, no curiosity in his gaze.

"It is finished," he said.

"Not yet." I reached for his hand and pulled him to his feet. He neither helped nor hindered me. His weight was like a sack of grain. But when I turned and started walking again, he didn't ask me to let him go. He walked with me.

Our steps were slow, though, too slow. I felt the land dragging at my feet. I wanted to stop, to gather my strength, just for a moment or two. Dust blew through the air, blurring my sight. My legs were lead, heavier than lead. Without realizing it I fell to my knees. Caleb's hand slipped from my own. I stared down at the blackened earth, knowing I needed to stand but not remembering how. Amid the cinders I saw dark maple seeds, gray mulberries, black acorns. I clutched a small dark nut in one hand — perfectly round, it belonged to no species I knew. Dead, I thought. Dead and gone. I was the one who had gone too far, beyond any place where things grew.

Yet the seed was cool in my hand. I felt the green deep within the nut calling me, begging to be called. Seeds weren't like people. Even when they seemed to sleep for years and years, something living remained in them, awaiting the call of sun and rain. Father had warned me often enough of the dangers seeds held.

But Father was gone. And the green in the nut kept calling me, begging to be called.

I remembered the green vines that had twined around Karin's hands. I remembered the weeds around our house and how they fought me year after year. I remembered how corn and squash fought me, fought my town and all its harvesting.

I clutched the nut tighter. I remembered how my town fought the corn and squash in turn, because we knew they would keep us alive. I remembered Matthew struggling to breathe as Caleb healed him. I remembered how tightly Allie had clutched the rope above her as she crossed the river.

I remembered how I'd called for Karin's help when the trees had attacked us. I remembered how I'd reached for Matthew's hand out of a dark river, because I knew without thought, without reason, that I, too, wanted to live.

I remembered Rebecca's cries. I remembered how my sister had come back at my call, clinging to shadow when nothing else remained. Most things wanted to grow, given a chance. I found the strength to *stand and reached for Caleb's hand once more. The seed in my other hand shivered, green struggling to break free. Around us the gray land turned to silver, shimmering bright. Silver surrounded us, veined everywhere with green —*

I blinked in the brightness, and all at once I was looking down at Caleb, and he was looking up at me, while Mom watched us both, tears drying on her cheeks. Caleb opened his mouth as if to speak, but no words came out. "I'm sorry," I said. My voice was stiff, as if not used to speech. "I know I should have asked. Allie says you should always ask before calling someone back. Only I can see well enough Mom needs you here, and Allie, too, so I couldn't just let you go. And, well, you didn't seem to mind, not like Tallow."

Caleb drew a long, uneven breath, then another, more steady. He sat up and solemnly lifted my chin. "Do not apologize, Liza. It was well done."

I cried then. Not for Mom, not for Caleb, not even for myself. For the memory of a seed, shivering in my hand, not understanding it was in a place without life or color or hope.

I realized I held something. I looked down, unfolding my fingers as I did.

A small red-brown nut lay cupped in my palm, perfectly round, save for a small crack in its shell, thin as good nylon thread from Before.

❧ Chapter 18 ❧

I had a sister once. She was a beautiful baby, long-limbed and graceful, eyes dark as shadows through mulberry trees.

A month after her birth I crept out before dawn. I followed the road, carrying an oil lamp in one hand. My breath frosted in front of me. Maples and sycamores whispered among themselves, but I didn't fear them. I listened, as Father had taught me always to listen. I knew I had magic enough to keep the trees at bay.

The hillside where Rebecca had died was a patchwork of blackberry and sumac. "*Go away,*" I whispered, and the bushes gently parted, letting me through.

I searched for a long time, but no bones remained, no sign that anything but brown roots had ever troubled the earth. Finally light touched the horizon, and I blew the lantern out. The sky was gray as old embers.

I opened my other hand and stared at the nut that lay in my palm. The crack in its shell remained small, but I felt the green within yearning, like the shadows of the dead had yearned, to be called.

I dug a hole in the dirt with my fingers and buried the nut there. "*Grow,*" I whispered to it. "*Seek sun, seek water, seek air.*"

I waited, but nothing happened. Sometimes what we want or don't want doesn't matter in the end. Sometimes magic doesn't listen after all. I patted the dirt down and returned to the road. I heard Allie's footsteps even before I turned. "You should know better by now than to leave us behind," she said. Her hand rested on a wolf's back; he'd been sniffing the ground as they walked. Allie drew her hand away, and the wolf sat, regarding me. I regarded him back, knowing his gray eyes. I would always know him, whatever form he took.

"I wasn't leaving," I said.

Allie tugged on her braid. Samuel had patiently worked all the tangles out. "That's what Matthew thought, too, but I wasn't so sure. So Matthew said he'd go with me, and Dad agreed. Boys aren't always silly, you know."

"I know." I reached out to scratch Matthew behind the ears, then drew away, embarrassed.

Matthew's nose nudged my hand back into place. Allie laughed. After a moment, I laughed, too. "You do have a wet nose," I said, kneeling to put my arms around his neck. Matthew rested his head on my shoulder with a contented sigh. I thought of how he'd followed me against all reason. A few snowflakes fell, and I watched them land in his fur. Maybe everything wasn't dust and ashes after all.

"Look!" Allie cried.

Reluctantly I drew away, looking where she pointed.

Amid the brambles of blackberry and sumac a green sapling rose from the hillside, sprouting branches, sprouting leaves, grasping for the sky. Even as I watched, the central shoot darkened to cinnamon brown. The green leaves grew bright, and brighter still, and then all at once green gave way to a brilliant orange-red—as if the leaves had caught a bit of sun and didn't want to let it go. Those leaves were perfectly round. Quia leaves. Leaves from Faerie.

Allie grabbed my hand. Beside us Matthew stood, ears cocked forward, fur bristling along his back. The tree kept growing until it was tall as I was, and taller still. The sumac and black-berry bushes around it began changing, too, their leaves catching shades of rust and scarlet. Suddenly frightened I shouted, "*Stop!*"

The quia tree grew on, heedless as the River of my command. A branch released an orange leaf. It fluttered to the ground. Wind blew another leaf toward the road. It landed in Allie's hair, and I hastily pulled it away.

The leaf wasn't warm, in spite of its fiery hue. It was a leaf, nothing more, nothing less. Other leaves began falling, too, doing no harm. Matthew caught one beneath his paw and sniffed it uneasily. The flurries stopped, but the air still smelled of snow.

Once leaves had changed color in autumn,

burning fierce as fire, falling soft as snow. I stared at the orange leaf in my hand, thinking of the seed I'd brought back from a place beyond either my world or Faerie, a place where the time for growing was past.

"I think it's all right," I said slowly. "I think it's only — autumn. The way autumn used to be Before."

For a time the tree kept growing and we kept watching it. At last the growing stopped. The quia stood tall as a young dogwood by then, and half its branches were bare. How long, I wondered, before new leaves started to grow? Not until the snows melted, perhaps.

A moment more I gazed at the hillside where my sister had died and where the quia tree now stood. "Rest well," I said softly, and then I turned away.

We returned to town in silence, watching the maples and elms catch color ahead of us, reds and yellows and oranges leaping from tree to tree, advancing through the forest, a fire without heat. Magic, I thought. Maybe there had always been something like magic in this world.

275

At the edge of town I hesitated, glancing at Matthew. He walked on without stopping, though, head and tail held high, as if he were done with hiding. I wondered whether that was safe, even with Father gone. But if anyone tried to harm him, they'd have both of us to answer to, and perhaps the others as well. Maybe in time we would all be able to stop hiding.

Most folks were out in the fields—the flurries were reminder enough of the need to finish harvesting. Outside Kate's home she and Samuel watched the changing leaves beyond the houses in silence, the door open behind them.

Samuel reached for his daughter as we approached. He hadn't let her out of his sight yesterday, not even when we went to bury Tallow. Allie had cried as I set the old cat down in the earth, even as she told me I was right to let Tallow go.

Now Allie solemnly handed her father a yellow oak leaf she'd picked up from the road. Samuel clutched it in his hand. "I think maybe the trees will sleep this winter." He grinned. "Almost like Before."

Allie laughed. "That's silly. Trees don't sleep."

Samuel tossed the leaf above him. It danced in the wind a moment before drifting down. Allie caught it again just before it touched the ground.

Behind them, Caleb stepped into the doorway. Mom followed, and Caleb helped her down the stairs. She was weak, she was pale, but she would heal now. Caleb had said so, and I was trying to believe it.

She wanted to heal now. I didn't need Caleb to tell me that.

At the bottom of the stairs Caleb drew away. He and Mom kept a careful distance, as if not quite sure of each other yet. I thought of how they'd walked together among the trees, un-afraid. But that was Before, and autumn or not, I doubted the trees would ever be fully tame again.

Caleb stared thoughtfully at the bright leaves. Then he stared at me, just as thoughtful. "Well done, indeed," he said, and nodded.

I held out the quia leaf in my hand.

Caleb grew very still. He took the leaf from me

as seriously as he had once taken a quarter from my mother, turning it over in his hands. "There'll be seeds," he said softly. "Within a few years. We'll go back then. We'll take the risk, if only long enough for planting." He smiled, a small smile but a real one, reminding me of the young man in my visions. "Our worlds have always been linked, Liza. We forgot that during the War. We should never have forgotten."

"Lizzy." Mom started forward, then stopped, as if no more sure of me than of Caleb.

I walked toward her instead, slowly, steadily — until with what might have been a sob and might have been a laugh she pulled me close.

All may yet be well. Almost, I believed that. Not as a promise. No one could promise, not after the War, not after so many other things that couldn't be undone.

But the trees were releasing their leaves. Who knew what else might happen?

Allie twirled her oak leaf on its stem. Matthew leaned against his grandmother, and Kate draped her arm absently over his back. Leaves continued to fall. Snow flurries began once more. And my mother kept holding me, holding me close, as if this time she wouldn't let go.

✌ Acknowledgments ✌

Many thanks to: Laurell K. Hamilton, Deborah Millitello, Marella Sands, Bob Sheaff, and Mark Sumner, who read the opening of Bones of Faerie before I left St. Louis; Jane Yolen, who also read the opening and kept asking when I was going to finish the book until I finally did; C. S. Adler, Dawn Dixon, Larry Hammer, Jill Knowles, Ann Manheimer, Patricia McCord, Earl W. Parrish, Roxy Rogers, Frances Robertson, Amy Stewart, Jennifer J. Stewart, and Robin Stewart, all of whom read and reread the manuscript for me; my agent, Nancy Gallt, who believed in the completed story; and Jim Thomas, editor of the original Random House edition, who took the best book I knew how to write and showed me how to make it better.

✌ About the Author ✌

Janni Lee Simner lives in the Arizona desert, where even without magic the plants know how to bite and the dandelions really do have thorns. *Bones of Faerie* is the first book of her *Bones of Faerie* trilogy.

Janni has also published the young adult fantasy *Thief Eyes,* four books for younger readers — most recently *Tiernay West, Professional Adventurer* — and more than 30 short stories. She's the author of the *Writing Life* series, and she wrote the script for Desert Owl Games' *The Huntsman: Winter's Curse.*

To learn more about Janni, visit her website at www.simner.com.

Faerie Winter

"Ethan!" My voice tightened around the call. I couldn't let him go. I had to know why he was afraid, and whether his magic had truly killed, and, if it had, how likely it was to kill again. *"Ethan, stop!"*

He jerked to a stop, just as I'd commanded. I felt the cold thread of my magic stretching between us.

Fear crept into his eyes. "You did that before, too, didn't you? Just like she did."

"Like who did?" I walked past Ethan, putting myself between him and the stairs. Matthew followed with the water basin.

"Let me go." Smoke rose from Ethan's bandages. "Let me go or I'll *kill* you, I swear it."

"Liza." There was a warning in Matthew's voice.

I ignored it, keeping my gaze and my magic focused on Ethan. "Like you killed Ben?"

Flames burst through Ethan's bandages. The magic binding him to me burned away as charred linen drifted to the floor. The boy drew his hands together, cupping a ball of fire within.

Matthew flung the water at him. The fire hissed but didn't go out. The scent of damp coals filled the air.

Matthew held the basin in front of us like a shield. "Easy, Ethan. We won't hurt you."

"*You* won't, maybe." Ethan's dark eyes reflected the fire he held. I felt its heat against my skin. Flames cast light onto the basin Matthew held. Brightness filled my sight—*No. Not now.* This was no time for visions. I tried to turn away, but it was too late. I had no choice but to see—

Cloaked figures following a river toward a town. One of them—a girl my age in a cloak the bright green of mulberry leaves—hesitated a moment, drawing back her hood to reveal long clear hair and bright silver eyes. Faerie eyes, I thought, and then I saw—

Flames consuming the town's houses. Snow sizzled as burning timbers crashed to the ground. Smoke billowed up and I saw—

Ethan watching the houses burn, the clear-haired girl's hand on his arm. She smiled at him, and he smiled back. Neither of them moved to stop the flames. Neither did the younger children arrayed around them. Those flames burned brighter, and by their glow I saw—

Fire leaping from cupped hands to catch at a

doorframe. Heat pulsed against my clothes and skin as wood burned —

Metal clattered as the basin hit the ground. Matthew grabbed my arm, and I realized these flames came from no vision. They were real, and they wreathed the doorway to Mom's room.

Faerie Winter excerpt © 2011 by Janni Lee Simner

Printed in Great Britain
by Amazon

54629269R00165